FLAVORS *under* THE BIG SKY

RECIPES AND STORIES FROM
YELLOWSTONE PUBLIC RADIO & BEYOND

STELLA FONG

PHOTOGRAPHY BY LYNN DONALDSON-VERMILLION
FOREWORD BY CHEF CHUCK SCHOMMER

AMERICAN PALATE

Published by American Palate
A Division of The History Press
Charleston, SC
www.historypress.com

Copyright © 2020 by Stella Fong
All rights reserved

First published 2020

Manufactured in the United States

ISBN 9781467144384

Library of Congress Control Number: 2020930495

Notice: The information in this book is true and complete to the best of our knowledge. It is offered without guarantee on the part of the author or The History Press. The author and The History Press disclaim all liability in connection with the use of this book.

All rights reserved. No part of this book may be reproduced or transmitted in any form whatsoever without prior written permission from the publisher except in the case of brief quotations embodied in critical articles and reviews.

CONTENTS

Foreword, by Chef Chuck Schommer	9
Acknowledgements	11
Introduction	15
PART I. STELLA'S MONTANA	25
PART II. RIVERS AND LAKES	61
PART III. MOUNTAINS	87
PART IV. PLAINS	121
PANTRY: SEASONINGS, SAUCES AND CONDIMENTS	193
Sources	213
Index	217
About the Author and Photographer	223

FOREWORD

One of the first times I met Stella Fong was at an event for the release of Greg Patent's James Beard Award–winning cookbook, *Baking in America*. It was 2002. We met because of our passion for food and our love of sharing this passion. Stella and I were both chefs, but on two very different paths. Stella was a writer and culinary educator who taught classes in a controlled environment to students paying her a fee to educate them. Me, I was an executive chef and also a culinary educator. However, it was in the controlled chaos of a hot restaurant kitchen.

My interest, like many other chefs, started in the family kitchen. My mother did the majority of the cooking, and she kept the family fed using the recipes that were handed down from generations. She was the keeper of the family recipe archive and did an excellent job adding her own special recipes. My father's specialty was breakfast, and he taught me the love of the smoker and sausage stuffer.

It was at the age of fifteen that I discovered that a restaurant kitchen was very different from my family's kitchen at home. Working in a commercial environment was hard work with long hours. I learned the importance of standardized recipes, preparing menu items the same way and that communication was key in running a successful shift. It was under the encouragement and guidance of the kitchen manager that I attended culinary school after graduating from high school in 1979. There, I was taught the basics, and it really opened my eyes. At this point, I knew I would someday own my own restaurant. Gaining experience, I worked at cafés, supper clubs, private clubs, guest ranches and steakhouses, honing my skills along the way. Buck's T-4 Lodge—a historic property in the Gallatin Canyon of Big Sky, Montana—was where I landed my first big chef's job. I was responsible for two outlets, three meal periods and a growing banquet business. We also ran a full-

FOREWORD

service hotel. I was scared to death. In 2011, my dream became a reality, and together with longtime co-worker David O'Connor, we purchased Buck's T-4 Lodge.

Looking back, the culinary scene in Montana in the early 1980s was very different from what it is today. Curly parsley was one of the only fresh herbs available. Most chefs didn't cook with local seasonal ingredients. The list of vegetables that grew best in the cold Montana climate was equally as short as the growing season. Thanks go to the many food entrepreneurs today who have helped extend the growing season and provide local Montana products on a more consistent basis. Foraging for quality ingredients for the culinary team is one of the most important hats a chef has to wear. You can't make great-tasting food if you don't start with quality ingredients.

This book is the result of being in search of quality ingredients and the love of teaching others how to use them. Today, the bounty in Montana is endless, and wild-foraged ingredients are common. In cooking, a person is only limited by their lack of imagination. Take the recipes from within, find great ingredients and enjoy sitting down at the table with family and friends.

—Chef Chuck Schommer

Chuck Schommer is co-owner and food and beverage director at Buck's T-4 Lodge in Big Sky. Schommer's culinary career has included a guest dinner at the prestigious James Beard Foundation in New York City, as well as national recognition in publications like the New York Times, Bon Appétit, Gourmet *and* Cooking Light. *He is often called on to represent Montana and Big Sky by such organizations as No Kid Hungry/Share Our Strength and the National Restaurant Associations ProStart program.*

ACKNOWLEDGEMENTS

Flavors Under the Big Sky would not have been possible without the help of so many people. I am in deep gratitude to my husband, Joe, for being my biggest taste tester and supporter. I thank him for bringing me to Montana to live under the big beautiful sky. I am forever in debt to my blonde sister Susan Carlson, who from the inception of this project offered her help in countless ways. Her husband, Gary, gets a shout-out too, as he is the man behind this great woman. I thank my true sister and her husband for coming to Billings from Arizona to help with a week of cooking—for Jana, undertaking the more challenging recipes, and endless dishwashing for John to complete the photoshoot. To the team that helped me cook my recipes—Lori Forseth, Rita Gallagher, Darla Jones, Leslie McCormick, Sandy Kunkel and Mary Underriner—I send immense gratitude. What a blessing to have artist Nancy Halter step in as the volunteer artistic director. She and her husband, ceramicist Greg Jahn, provided most of the serveware from their personal collection for the pictures. I thank Valeria Jeffries and Marti Miller for their brainstorming ideas for dish presentation and the loan of dishware. To Sean McDaniel, I thank you for modeling for the manly shots in the book, as well as your generous words of encouragement. I thank Cindy Smith for her enthusiasm and kindness in testing and tasting recipes. To John Wilson and his children, Liv and Dax, thank you also for input and recipe testing. In the Emerald City, I send thanks to Mark and Diane Cushing for Mark's cooking and Diane's tasting. I appreciate organizational help from Suzi Rietz and Jolyn Sweitzer for stepping in at the last minute to help with the final recipes.

I thank my dear culinary friend Robin Kline for her ideas, edits and recipe testing. She was the first person I called for advice and direction when I received the contract for this

ACKNOWLEDGEMENTS

book. Always I am appreciative of the support from my food partner Terrie Chrones, who has been at my side since the beginning of my culinary pursuits.

At Yellowstone Public Radio, I am in debt to Ken Siebert, program manager, who was a constant sounding board for me with ideas and possibilities for this cookbook. His production assistance and advice with my radio show, *Flavors Under the Big Sky*, have been invaluable. I thank Sarah Brown, host of *Field Days*, for her edits of my headnotes and stories. I am grateful to Kay Erickson, host of *All Things Considered*, for the sharing of every topic on food. Thank you to News Director Nicky Ouellet for always flavorful support. To the crew at YPR, thank you for tasting the concoctions I created. I thank Jackie Yamanaka for bringing me to Yellowstone Public Radio.

I thank Harper and Madison for allowing me to make my second office at their counter. To Joanie Swords, Pam Kemmick, Dimitra Moser, Keller Paulson, Alisha Lombard and the crew at this neighborhood gem, thank you for nurturing and nourishing me. I am grateful to Renee Coppock for her edits and being a constant sounding board for my ideas. I thank Chef Chuck Schommer of Buck's T-4 for being such a culinary hero and inspiration for me and Montana. Finally, I feel privileged to have worked with the very talented Lynn Donaldson-Vermillion, who has enhanced my writings in her column, "The Last Best Plates"; my blog for Yellowstone Public Radio; and the recipes in this cookbook with her amazing photographs.

Flavors Under the Big Sky would not have been possible without the expert support from editors Artie Crisp and Ryan Finn at The History Press. Thank you for your countless ideas and unrelenting patience.

I thank all those people who have shared their food stories with me from under the biggest and most beautiful sky. Mostly I thank those listeners who have tuned in every third Monday night at 6:30 p.m. all these years to help celebrate the bounty of the region.

INTRODUCTION

*F*lavors Under the Big Sky: Recipes and Stories from Yellowstone Public Radio & Beyond and the radio show that gave rise to it, *Flavors Under the Big Sky: Celebrating the Bounty of the Region*, are my homage to Montana and to all the people who have shared their food stories with me. This book reflects the evolution of my cooking after moving to Billings from San Diego twenty years ago. It is a small representation of the food I now cook after unearthing the bounty available here. This is a cookbook where I took Montana basics and created a world of flavors. Let this book be one you use over and over when you cook under the Big Sky and elsewhere.

FLAVORS UNDER THE BIG SKY: CELEBRATING THE BOUNTY OF THE REGION

Hosting a radio show was never on the list of the things I wanted to pursue in my lifetime. In fact, I was very uncomfortable with my voice when I was younger, and only in recent years have I accepted the way I speak. Nevertheless, after my first book, *Historic Restaurants of Billings: A Taste of the Magic City's Past*, came out in 2016, Yellowstone Public Radio's then news director, Jackie Yamanaka, called to ask me to develop a show. That conversation led me to take on the best job I have ever had.

I feel honored to hear people's stories about their connection to food. Even the quietest people have something to tell, an idea to share or an opinion on the topic of food. Food is the ingredient for people to stir up their thoughts. It brings memories and

INTRODUCTION

opinions to a simmer. Everyone can talk about what they ate for breakfast. There are always insights into favorite restaurants or what was savored for dinner the night before. Food bakes up stories about family and friends. Sometimes, food cooks up topics that are difficult to talk about.

I am grateful to all the people I have interviewed for *Flavors Under the Big Sky*, but I want to mention those who have most influenced my cooking and inspired the recipes for this book. Chef Sean Sherman, author of *The Sioux Chef's Indigenous Kitchen*, shined the brightest light on the bounty of this region, showcasing food under the Big Sky in its most natural form. To this day, I cannot believe Trevor McFerrin took me out to hunt for the elusive morel mushroom. I learned about eating insects from Dr. Florence Dunkel and Chef Joseph Yoon at the Second Annual Bug Cookoff at Montana State University. After tasting lemony black ants and nutty grasshoppers, I went to visit Cowboy Cricket Farms in Belgrade. YPR program director Ken Siebert and I will never forget how we were greeted with the intoxicating aroma of butter and sugar when we stepped into the storefront and production facility of Béquet Confections to interview founder and owner Robin Béquet.

I marvel at the producers who grow the bounty we bring to the table. Kate Rosetto of Kate's Garden tirelessly works her one and one-third acres in the Billings Heights to grow specialty items for her Community Supported Agriculture (CSA) subscribers and local chefs. Shelli Gayvert, a longtime Yellowstone Valley Farmers' Market board member, is one of the strongest behind-the-scenes leaders of this invaluable resource for fresh fruits and vegetables. I will never forget the infectious enthusiasm of twelve-year-old Phillip Prewett, who came to the market with his family to sell the produce they grew on their Park City farm. More recently, mother-daughter team Ronna Klamert and Veronnaka Evenson of Swanky Roots started an aquaponics system that now supplies fresh lettuce and microgreens year-round.

Claudia Krevat of Claudia's Mesa renewed my love of legumes. She has worked with organic farmers David Oien, Jim Barngrover, Tom Hastings and Bud Barta from Timeless Natural Food to spread information on the benefits of lentils. Her Colombian-inspired seasonings nudged me to revisit some recipes I had not cooked for some time using Montana-grown black beluga lentils, purple barley and black chickpeas.

I went to the American Fork Ranch in Two Dot to learn about sustainable practices for raising healthy cattle. Shane and Tanya Flowers of Ranch House Sausage Company provided insight on how meat is processed for consumers to buy in nice packages at the grocery store or sourced to chefs like Nick Steen of Walkers Grill. I learned more about the preparation techniques that Chefs David Maplethorpe of The Rex and Austin Stewart of Buffalo Block use for their diners.

INTRODUCTION

My visits to the Gallatin River Lodge outside Bozeman, The Ranch at Rock Creek in Phillipsburg and Chico Hot Springs in Pray renewed my love of fly fishing. Chefs Scott Meyers and Joshua Drage act as ambassadors in highlighting the bounty of the region. Chef Dave Wells at Chico Hot Springs elevates local cuisine by using world flavors in food he serves in the intimate six-seat Tasting Room.

I learned from Chef Bill Baskin, Gallatin College MSU culinary arts director, about his favorite local haunts. He introduced me to Andleeb Dawood of Saffron Table, who in her captivating sing-song voice told me about the flavors of her Pakistani childhood that she now shares in her restaurant. Together, Chef Baskin and I tasted southern fried chicken from the Roost and bibimbap from Whistle Pig Korean. These visits inspired me to revisit recipes I had not cooked for some time.

Billings is my home turf, and I am proud of the pioneers who have made our city more flavorful. Gary Brockel and his daughter, Jodi, run Brockel's Chocolates, the confectionery store that opened more than four decades ago and is an icon in downtown Billings. More recently, Clint Peck of Yellowstone Cellars and Winery brought his ranching tenacity to making wine from grapes he personally collects from Washington. The Patel family relocated from Bozeman to bring vegetarian Indian cuisine to Montana's Trailhead. And downtown, Veronika Baukema opened Veronika's Pastry Shop, an eastern European and French bakery, while François Morin opened Le Fournil, a traditional French bread bakery. Chef Nick Steen of Walkers Grill, the latest James Beard Foundation semifinalist for Best Chef of the Mountain Region, a new category, constantly pushes the envelop.

I am grateful to Chefs James Honaker of Bistro Enzo and Jeremy Engebretson of Lilac, both of Billings, and Red Lodge's Mike Muirhead of Mas Taco—all James Beard Foundation semifinalists for Best Chef of the Northwest—for highlighting food at its best with superior cooking techniques and passion. Honaker's expertise is seafood, while Muirhead's is Mexican cuisine. Engebretson captivates diners with trending styles and excels at pairing wine and beer with food. His partnerships with Carter's Brewing's Michael Ulrich in Billings, KettleHouse Brewing Company in Missoula and other Montana brewers help spotlight Montana's growing brewing business.

Jimmy Li of Fancy Sushi Asian Fusion brings Asian flavors to Billings and the ingredients of hard work. His food recalls the dishes I grew up with in the Bay Area and lived near as an adult in San Diego. Jimmy and his wife, Icy, remind me of my hardworking Chinese parents who put in long hours at our family's grocery store in Berkeley in the San Francisco Bay Area.

INTRODUCTION

MY CHINESE BACKGROUND

I do not recall deep conversations with my Chinese-born parents. My father and mother expressed the care and love they held for my siblings and me through food. They were unable to express their emotions in any other way. My aunts stuffed us with cakes and dumplings rather than filling our heads with the worries of the world. When my relatives greeted one another near dinner time, they would ask, "Have you eaten rice?" instead of "How are you doing?"

My father, Man Kin, immigrated to Hong Kong from Canton, China, in the early 1950s after the Communists founded the People's Republic of China. As a high school teacher, my father knew he would be challenged as an educated individual and slipped out from the south to start a new life in Hong Kong. He left before his mother. Weeks later, she packed some clothes into a shopping bag and departed in the dark of night to join her son in Hong Kong.

My husband, Joe, and I took my parents to visit my father's home in the late 1990s, forty years after he left it. When the Chinese took over his family's property, they confiscated the family's lychee fields but left the house alone. For years, it remained in the possession of a cousin. She kept the key and left the house as it was.

Two padlocked doors secured the space about the size of a large garage. About half an inch of dust covered the floor. What was left behind remained mostly untouched all those years. My father's childhood books remained in a bookcase. In the kitchen, by the sink, a dish rack held chopsticks and overturned rice bowls.

My father was the youngest of eleven children—four girls and seven boys. He had the opportunity to be with his mother and helped her cook. Dad brought that love of food and cooking to our family.

My father met my mother, Chor Man, in Hong Kong, where she was teaching kindergarten. In the three years they courted before they married, they laid the plans to relocate to the United States. They landed on Gold Mountain (the name given to America in Chinese) in San Francisco in 1956.

While my mother had to learn how to cook the basics when she first arrived, my father cured duck, fried whole fish and stir-fried crabs. He dried beef jerky flavored with soy sauce, sesame oil and brown sugar directly on the racks of our gas oven. He invented concoctions with boxed mashed potatoes and curry powder and incorporated SPAM into fried rice and steamed eggs. Working in a grocery store, Dad had access to many new food products, so I grew up with instant chocolate breakfast drink combined with Chinese rice porridge and instant oatmeal mixed with mushroom soup and green onions. In this cookbook, I share a few recipes inspired by my father's culinary curiosity.

INTRODUCTION

MY OWN FOOD JOURNEY

Fast-forward to college, when I finally had to cook for myself as a student at the University of California–Davis. I asked my father to write down recipes for the dishes he made, but he always said he couldn't. Dad sensed his food, seeing how cooked meat should look, hearing the hot oil dance in the wok, tasting how much a dish needed to be seasoned and smelling for the freshness of fish. He was always meticulous, especially when he sliced his stir-fry vegetables. As I watched him, I imagined he had a ruler next to a stem of bok choy or stalks of green onions as he made precise cuts.

For several evenings, I stood by my father at the stovetop and scribbled frantically on a notebook to record the magic he was performing in the wok. I managed to make some smoke and needed some mirrors in the ensuing years, but it was not until I met Lily Loh many years later that I got the specific instructions I needed to really pull a rabbit out of the hat.

Lily Loh, cooking teacher and author of *Chinese Seafood and Vegetables*, took me under her wing and mentored me when I first started teaching cooking classes. When the Food Network began in the early 1990s, cooking stores were inspired to offer cooking lessons. Suddenly everyone wanted to learn how to cook. In San Diego, I taught at several outlets, but working with Lily solidified the Chinese cooking I grew up with. She wrote down recipes in detail. To this day, I use her recipes as the backbones of recipes I have modified for my kitchen.

We collaborated for an article for *Cooking Light* magazine on stir-frying meats and vegetables. From there, I began writing articles for the *San Diego Union Tribune*, *Fine Cooking* and the *Washington Post* and teaching in the San Diego and Los Angeles areas.

I earned a cooking certificate from the Culinary Institute of America in Hyde Park, New York, and Greystone in Napa, California. Because most of my cooking had been learned from my father, I wanted to be sure I had more extensive culinary knowledge. However, I mostly taught traditional Asian-style cooking classes for the local cooking schools.

INTRODUCTION

MAKING THE MOVE TO MONTANA

When Joe and I first moved to Billings from San Diego in June 1999, I had the opportunity to instruct for Sur La Table in Seattle, Scottsdale and Los Angeles. In the cold of winter, I found reprieve from the frigid Montana temperatures, but more importantly, the travel brought me to cities where I could stock up my Billings pantry. I shipped boxes of foodstuffs and wine, believing I would wither away if I did not have the goods I was used to cooking with in San Diego. I looked forward to the brown truck arriving at my front door.

Early on, I shipped the basics to make seasoning and sauce combinations. I would always have salt fermented black soybeans in my refrigerator. In my pantry, soy sauce, sesame oil, dry sherry and dried chili peppers were always on hand. Fresh ginger was harder to come by, so I smuggled the rhizomes home in my suitcase as often as I could. Star anise, Sichuan peppercorns and turmeric powder lived in my spice drawer, transported from a bigger city.

But then something changed. In writing *Historic Restaurants of Billings* and *Billings Food: The Flavorful Story of Montana's Trailhead*, I discovered what a treasure of flavors and talents the city I now called home possessed. Early menus presented diverse offerings: The Rex served charcuterie and oysters; the Luzon had perch, salmon and black bass; and the St. Louis Café, a 24/7 eatery, offered shrimp and lobster salad, as well as raw oysters and fresh smelt and halibut.

CELEBRATING MONTANA

The book is divided into five main chapters. "Stella's Montana" will showcase recipes from San Diego and those inspired by my father and mother. The rest of the bulk of the book will be divided geographically—"Rivers and Lakes," "Mountains" and "Plains." Since I live in the plains, this section will be the largest and fullest. The plains are where agriculture dominates. Trout live in the rivers and lakes, while planted Pacific salmon, Chinook, can be found in Fork Peck Reservoir in the northeast corner of the state. Western lakes like Flathead harbor cherry and peach trees. Morels and asparagus can be found near the rivers. I include several recipes for game such as elk, duck and bison. Early on, Joe hunted pheasant, and we had the chance to savor the local bounty. Finally, in "Pantry: Seasonings, Sauces and Condiments," recipes for basic flavorings are included that can be used in several recipes in this book.

INTRODUCTION

Each chapter is divided into two rough sections, themed as "Foraged & Hunted" and "Harvested & Collected." In the former, the key ingredient in the dish requires searching and hunting over the landscape under the Big Sky to bring it into the kitchen and to the table. In the latter, the highlighted ingredient is brought to the kitchen after its selection at its prime and then cooked and savored at the table. The food comes from home gardeners, local farmers or producers or from large commercial sources. The key ingredients are those that are indigenous or can grow well in this region.

In many of the recipes, the bold text in the ingredients lists or introductions refers to a specific recipe within the index. Many of the references are the sauces or spices I developed early on in creating the world pantry I use to cook with.

This cookbook and the radio show are testaments to the people who produce and cook here under the Big Sky. Thank you to all of you who have shared the bounty and deliciousness of this region with me.

PART I
STELLA'S MONTANA

This section holds the recipes inspired from when I first moved here, bringing many of the ways I was cooking accompanied with the seasonings and spices. This was the period when I was not fully aware of what abounded in Montana, and foods from around the world were not as readily available. The recipes are reminiscent of my childhood. Although the recipes may not be the exact dishes my father or mother cooked, they were inspired by them.

ROAST DUCK WITH STEAMED BUNS

SERVES 2

Duck has always been my favorite "red" meat. I love chicken cooked every which way, and duck is just like a cross between chicken and beef. The Steamed Buns and Homemade Hoisin Sauce are good accompaniments to this duck. However, it can be sliced and served on the side of the Butter Lettuce Salad.

*For wild duck, use the marinade and then sear the breasts on a hot pan or on the grill, cooking just enough to brown or make good grill marks on each side. Wild duck has less fat and you cannot render the fat to get a crispy skin. In addition, wild duck breasts are thinner than those from farmed duck and do not need to be finished in the oven. Duck breast is best served medium rare. However, it can be sliced and served on the side of the **Butter Lettuce Salad** or stuffed into **Mandarin Pancakes**.*

FOR THE MARINADE

2 tablespoons **Homemade Hoisin Sauce**

2 tablespoons dry sherry

¼ teaspoon **Five-Spice Powder**

2 tablespoons minced ginger
(about a 1-by-1-inch piece, peeled)

2 cloves garlic, minced

¼ teaspoon salt

2 duck breasts, about 8 ounces each

In a bowl, stir together all the marinade ingredients. Add duck breasts and coat the outsides thoroughly with marinade. Marinate for at least an hour in the refrigerator or preferably overnight.

Heat oven to 425°F.

Remove duck breasts from marinade, discarding marinade and patting breasts dry with paper towels. Score the skin half an inch apart in a diamond pattern, being careful not to score the meat.

Place the duck breasts skin side down in a heavy, ovenproof skillet. Cook over medium heat until meat starts to sizzle. Turn to medium-low heat. Cook until skin turns golden brown, about 10 to 12 minutes. If skin starts to burn, turn the heat even lower. Flip the breast every 3 to 4 minutes.

Transfer pan to the oven with breast skin side down. Bake for about 5 minutes for medium-rare (when the internal temperature reaches 135°F) or to your desired doneness.

STEAMED BUNS

MAKES 16 BUNS

When we moved to Montana, these were the breads I missed the most. Living in San Diego, I often went to Clairemont Mesa, where there were Asian restaurants and markets. With friends I ventured out for dim sum, a style of Chinese eating where small plates are brought to the table in carts pushed by women shouting the name of goodies they were selling. Steamed buns were usually stuffed with barbecue pork or sweetened bean paste. This recipe is for the plain buns, which can accompany Korean Beef, meat shredded from Garlic, Thyme and Sage Baked Chicken or, best, Roasted Duck Breast. For me, I would eat these buns plain, right out of the steamer, but they are delectable with some Homemade Hoisin Sauce and shredded green onions.

parchment paper
2 teaspoons active dry yeast
¼ cup whole milk
½ cup water
2¼ cups flour plus extra for dusting
3 tablespoons sugar
½ teaspoon salt
¼ teaspoon baking powder
¼ teaspoon baking soda
sesame oil

COOK'S NOTES

Buns can be stored in the freezer in an airtight container. To reheat, set in steamer for about 30 minutes until fluffy, soft and heated through.

Cut sixteen 3-inch parchment squares. Set aside. In a small bowl, whisk together yeast, milk and water. Set aside.

In a medium bowl, stir together flour, sugar, salt, baking powder and baking soda. Make a well in the middle of the flour and pour in the yeast mixture. With a spatula, bring flour and liquid together until a dough forms. Add a little more water if the dough is too dry. Knead dough with your hands to incorporate all the flour. Turn dough onto a lightly floured surface and knead until dough is smooth and elastic, about 10 minutes. Dough will be stiff. Place dough in a lightly oiled bowl, cover with plastic wrap and let rise until double, about 1 hour.

Line a baking sheet with parchment paper.

Punch dough down and turn it out onto a clean surface. Roll dough into a long log, about 12 inches, and cut into 4 pieces. Gently roll each piece into logs and cut each log into 4 equal-size pieces. Roll each piece into a ball and place on baking sheet. Cover with plastic wrap and let rise for 30 minutes.

Roll each ball into a 3-inch round and brush top with sesame oil. Fold in half, with oiled side on the inside. Let rest for 30 minutes.

Set up steamer on top of the stove. Working in batches, steam the buns on the parchment squares, making sure the breads do not touch one another and allowing for further expansion during cooking, leaving at least ½ inch in spacing. Steam for 10 minutes. Serve immediately.

STEAMED WHOLE TROUT WITH GINGER AND GARLIC

SERVES 2 TO 4

My visits to the Gallatin River Lodge outside Bozeman, The Ranch at Rock Creek in Phillipsburg and Chico Hot Springs in Pray renewed my love of fly fishing. Chefs Scott Meyers, Joshua Drage and Dave Wells act as ambassadors in showcasing the bounty of the region.

Cooking freshly caught river trout is special. When I was backpacking, I would bring aluminum foil, ginger root and some garlic cloves along with a small bottle of sesame oil and some salt. I would coat the foil with some oil, put the fish in the clean foil and then sprinkle on some chopped ginger and garlic. The wrapped fish would go directly into the coals of the fire. After opening up the package, I would sprinkle a little salt on. Nothing tasted more delicious!

1½ pounds fresh whole trout, cleaned, guts and scales removed
salt and fresh ground pepper, to taste
3 tablespoons unsalted butter, at room temperature
2 large shallots, sliced
⅓ cup 1-inch long julienned ginger
⅓ cup sliced garlic
1 tablespoon sesame oil

FOR SAUCE

2 teaspoons sesame oil
¼ to ½ teaspoon chili flakes
3 tablespoons balsamic vinegar
¼ cup soy sauce
4 stalks green onions, sliced diagonally

Heat oven to 425°F. Tear off enough aluminum foil to wrap the fish loosely, leaving enough room above and around the fish for steaming when it is cooking. Set aside.

With a sharp knife, make diagonal cuts into the fish just to the bones about 2 inches apart, starting at the stomach area down to the tail. Sprinkle with salt and pepper, to taste. Press pieces of butter into the cuts and spread about 1 tablespoon butter into the abdominal cavity. With remaining butter, spread onto the bottom of the foil to just beyond the footprint of the fish.

Sprinkle half the shallots on top of the butter, followed with half the ginger and garlic. Place fish on top of mixture. Stuff some ginger and garlic into the stomach of the fish. Sprinkle remaining shallots, ginger and garlic on top of the fish. Drizzle with sesame oil.

Wrap foil tightly around the fish leaving about 1 inch above the fish and to the sides. Bake for 25 to 30 minutes or until meat of fish is flakey.

Just before fish is done, heat sesame oil in a small saucepan. Add chili flakes and cook for about 30 seconds. Add vinegar and soy sauce and bring to a simmer.

When fish is done, sprinkle green onions on top and then drizzle about half of the sauce over the fish. Serve immediately with the remaining sauce.

PHEASANT STIR-FRY WITH BLACK BEAN SAUCE

SERVES 4 TO 6

Our first hunting experiences were with friends Wiley and Marilyn Bland in North Dakota. Our English setter, Mancha, pointed many a pheasant for my husband to bring home. This recipe from my collection worked beautifully with this newly discovered meat.

During hunting season, elk or grouse can easily be substituted in this stir-fry recipe. You might also consider using chicken, pork, beef or shrimp. Use any black beans you may have left over from making the Homemade Hoisin Sauce to make this luscious dish. The recipe for Black Bean Sauce is found in the "Pantry" section of this cookbook. If you do not have black beans, finish the dish with a drizzle of soy sauce and sesame oil.

1 pound pheasant breast, cut into ½-inch dice

FOR THE MARINADE
2 tablespoons soy sauce
1 tablespoon dry sherry
1 tablespoon cornstarch

1 tablespoon plus 1 tablespoon canola or vegetable oil, divided
1 red pepper, stems and seeds removed, large diced
Black Bean Sauce
2 green onions, diagonally sliced

In a bowl, mix pheasant with marinade ingredients. Marinate in refrigerator for at least 30 minutes or overnight. Heat 1 tablespoon oil in wok or large skillet over medium-high heat. Add pheasant and stir-fry until browned and cooked through, no longer pink in the middle, about 3 minutes. Scoop pheasant out of pan and set aside on a plate. Add remaining oil into the hot pan, add red peppers and stir-fry for about 1 minute until peppers are just softened. Scoop out peppers and place on plate with pheasant. Bring sauce to a boil. Stir in pheasant, peppers and green onions. Stir-fry for 1 minute or until heated through. Serve immediately.

FLAVORS UNDER THE BIG SKY

BROWN BUTTER FIVE-SPICE APPLE TART

MAKES ONE TART

The best tart is made from those small Montana apples, as they have a good balance of sweetness and tartness. So many apple trees line the sidewalks in Billings that in the fall, apples litter the streets. I am always saddened that so much bounty goes to waste. If you want a bit more decadence, accompany this dessert with the addition of caramel sauce made from Béquet Confections. Melt 8 ounces of caramels with a little water and then add some half and half to make a luscious sauce to slather over the tart.

FOR THE CRUST

1 cup all-purpose flour
1 teaspoon sugar
pinch of salt
6 tablespoons unsalted butter, cut into ½-inch pieces
3½ tablespoons ice water

FOR THE FILLING

2 tablespoons unsalted butter
½ teaspoon **Five-Spice Powder**
2 pounds gala, Granny Smith or your favorite apples, peeled, cored and sliced

1 egg
1 teaspoon water
3 tablespoons sugar or to desired sweetness

WITH FOOD PROCESSOR:

In a food processor, add the flour, sugar and salt. Pulse to combine. Add the butter and pulse until the dough forms pieces that look like large peas. Add water and pulse until the dough comes together.

BY HAND:

Add flour, sugar and salt to a medium bowl and stir together to combine. Add butter and squeeze butter and flour together with your thumbs until the dough resembles large peas. Add the water 1 tablespoon at a time and let the water absorb. Toss the dough with hands, letting it fall through your fingers until it is ropy. If there are dry flour patches, add a little bit more water. Keep tossing until the dough appears to come together. Press into a disk, about 7 inches in diameter. Wrap in plastic wrap and refrigerate for at least 1 hour or overnight.

Heat oven to 400°F. Line a baking sheet with parchment paper and set aside.

In a small pan, melt butter over medium-high heat. After butter melts, cook for another 2 minutes to brown the butter but not to burn. Pour butter into a small bowl, mix with five-spice powder and set aside.

On a lightly floured surface, roll the crust to a diameter about 12 inches, about ⅛ inch thick. Place on the lined baking sheet. Overlap apples on the dough in a ring about 2 inches from the edge. Continue inward until the center is reached. Drizzle butter over apples. Fold the dough edges over apples.

In a small bowl, beat the egg with 1 teaspoon of water. Brush the egg wash on the folded edges. Dust with sugar over the filling and edges.

Bake in the center of the oven until apples are soft and edges are golden brown, about 1 hour. If edges get too brown, cover with aluminum foil. Remove tart from the oven and allow to cool for about 15 minutes. Slice and serve.

KUNG PAO PORK WITH RED CHILIES AND PEANUTS

SERVES 4 TO 6

Lily Loh, Chinese cookbook author, cooking teacher and my mentor, inspired this recipe. She perfected one of the favorite dishes I enjoyed as a child when my family went to Chinese restaurants. I just loved the bold flavors from the seasonings of fresh ginger and dried chili peppers. Dad never made this dish at home because my mother did not care for hot spiciness.

I brought the recipe to Billings and found it perfect for the game we were being introduced to. Pheasant was the first game my husband brought home with our first hunting dog, MacKenzie. Although Mack was a hunting school dropout because of his laidback attitude, he still managed to point Joe to a few birds. If you have pheasant, grouse or elk, this recipe is perfect for cooking up your bounty.

1 pound pork tenderloin, cut into ½-inch cubes
1 tablespoon cornstarch
1 tablespoon soy sauce
2 tablespoons plus 1 tablespoon canola or vegetable oil, divided
8 dried chili peppers, stems, tips and seeds removed
1 teaspoon minced ginger
1 red pepper, stem and seeds removed, cut into ½-inch dice
½ cup unsalted roasted peanuts

FOR THE SAUCE

2 tablespoons soy sauce
1 tablespoon dry sherry
1 tablespoon sugar
½ tablespoon dark vinegar
1 teaspoon cornstarch
1 teaspoon sesame oil
½ teaspoon salt

In a medium bowl, mix pork with cornstarch and soy sauce and marinate for at least 30 minutes or overnight.

Heat 2 tablespoons of oil in a wok or skillet over medium-high heat. Stir-fry pork for about 2 minutes until just browned. Scoop pork out of pan and set aside on a plate. (Be sure to turn on your exhaust fans to remove the spicy fumes.) Fry chili peppers in remaining oil over medium-high heat until they turn black. Add ginger and red pepper and stir over high heat for a few seconds. Scoop out and place on plate with pork.

In a medium bowl, combine sauce ingredients. Make sure the cornstarch is dissolved before cooking. Bring sauce to a boil and until thickened. Add pork back into sauce along with bell pepper and chili peppers. Stir in peanuts and heat for 1 minute. Serve immediately.

KOREAN BEEF

SERVES 4 TO 8

I was reminded of the deliciousness of this dish when I visited Whistle Pig Korean, owned by Emma Woods and Ross Franklin, in Bozeman with Chef Bill Baskin, culinary arts director at Gallatin College MSU. Korean beef goes with everything. It can be sandwiched between a brioche bun, served on top of rice noodles or white rice or mounded onto mashed potatoes.

I recommend using a wok because it's roomy, but a cast-iron skillet works just fine. Also, you can grill this meat. Just be sure to spray the grill with cooking spray. I basically sear the meat, as I love my meat on the medium rare side.

Gochujang is a deep crimson–colored paste the consistency of thick peanut butter. It is the everyday go-to seasoning in Korean cooking. If you cannot get the fermented paste made with red chili powder, glutinous rice, salt and fermented soybeans, puree canned chipotle peppers as a substitute. However, keep in mind this will add smokiness and hotness to the meat. Otherwise, chili flakes with soy sauce and a little sugar can be an adequate replacement.

FOR THE MARINADE

2 tablespoons minced ginger

6 garlic cloves, minced

½ Asian apple, peeled, cored, finely chopped

2 tablespoons Gochujang paste

3 tablespoons dark brown sugar

1 tablespoon sesame oil

⅓ cup soy sauce

1 tablespoon mirin

3 pounds beef chuck, thinly sliced

3 tablespoons or more canola oil

Mix together the marinade ingredients in a large bowl. Add the meat and make sure sauce covers all of the meat. Marinate in refrigerator for at least 2 hours and best overnight.

Heat about 1 tablespoon oil in a wok over medium-high heat until oil smokes slightly. Spread beef slices out onto the hot surface to brown, about 1 to 2 minutes. Turn beef and cook on other side to desired doneness, about 1 to 2 minutes. Scoop meat out onto a plate. Continue cooking the rest of the meat.

COOK'S NOTES

No Asian apple? Use pear, peeled, cored and stem removed. No Gochujang? Try canned chipotle peppers, but keep in mind that these peppers may be spicier and definitely smokier in flavor.

GRILLED FLANK STEAK WITH ASIAN CHIMICHURRI SAUCE

SERVES 4 WITH ABOUT 1¼ CUPS SAUCE

Chimichurri sauce can be used on just about any meat, but I believe it is best with beef—and of course, beef is Montana's pride. If you want to use seafood, go with a more robust fish such as halibut or salmon, or even shrimp, all of which will hold up to the full-flavored sauce.

Best of all, thin slices of this leftover steak are delicious put between corn tortillas with some fresh tomatoes, avocado, lettuce and a drizzle of chimichurri sauce or sandwiched between two pieces of bread slathered with sauce, a little mayonnaise and a handful of spinach leaves.

In the winter, this sauce brings hope of spring with its bright-green color and herbaceous flavors. My husband will heat up a grill outside to cook this steak. Otherwise, broil the meat, making sure to place it at least 4 inches away from the heat. Keep the oven door open about 2 or 3 inches and watch the meat as it browns. The meat thermometer will be the main indicator of how your beef is cooking.

FOR THE SEASONING

½ teaspoon chili powder

½ teaspoon salt

¼ teaspoon fresh ground black pepper

1½ pounds flank steak

FOR THE SAUCE

2 cups fresh cilantro

1 cup fresh parsley

2 green onions, coarsely chopped

4 cloves garlic

½ jalapeño, stem and seeds removed

¼ cup balsamic vinegar

1 tablespoon soy sauce

1 tablespoon fresh lime juice

½ cup extra virgin olive oil

In a small bowl, stir together the seasoning ingredients. Rub both sides of steak with seasoning and let rest at room temperature for 30 minutes.

Into a food processor, add all the sauce ingredients and pulse until cilantro and parsley are finely chopped. Remove to a medium bowl, cover and let rest at room temperature for about 1 hour to allow flavors to meld.

Heat grill to high. Place steak on the grill and cook until nicely charred, 4 to 5 minutes. Turn and grill about 2 to 3 minutes more for medium-rare (an internal temperature of about 135°F), 5 to 7 minutes for medium (140°F) or 8 to 10 minutes for medium-well (150°F).

Transfer steak to a plate or cutting board, tent loosely with foil and let rest for 5 minutes before slicing to serve with chimichurri sauce.

RACK OF LAMB IN CURRY HOISIN SAUCE

SERVES 2 AS AN ENTRÉE

For those who do not care for lamb, these chops may just change their minds. I have been serving this dish for years because it is easy and tasty. I marinate the chops the night before and have the lamb on a lined baking sheet with the oven preheating as the guests arrive. Then, like clockwork, the chops cook to medium rare in 20 minutes. This recipe uses **Homemade Hoisin Sauce** *and* **Curry Powder** *from the "Pantry" chapter, but go ahead and use store-purchased sauce and seasoning if that is what you have.*

1 rack of Frenched lamb ribs
   (about 2 pounds)

FOR THE MARINADE

4 cloves garlic, minced

4 tablespoons **Homemade Hoisin Sauce**

2 tablespoons honey

2 tablespoons soy sauce

1 tablespoon sesame oil

2 teaspoons garlic chili sauce

1 tablespoon **Curry Powder**

2 teaspoons fresh ground black pepper

Trim fat off rack of ribs if necessary. Set aside. In a large bowl, mix together marinade ingredients. Add lamb and spoon marinade to cover meat. Marinate for at least 2 hours or, better, overnight.

Heat oven to 425°F. Line baking sheet with foil. Place lamb rack with meat side up on the sheet pan. Bake for 15 to 20 minutes until meat thermometer inserted in the thickest part registers 145°F for medium-rare doneness. Let the meat rest for 5 minutes. Slice rack into chops and serve immediately.

CURRY MASHED POTATOES

SERVES 8

For me, these potatoes hold fond memories of my father and how he used to experiment with new recipes. He used the off-the-shelf curry powder from the Indo-European spice company and baked russet potatoes or sometimes potato flakes. He spread the mashed potatoes onto soft white bread with the crusts trimmed off. He then sprinkled chopped green onions on top and browned everything under the broiler. I like spreading the potatoes on a croissant and sprinkling green onions on top like Dad did, followed with some grated mozzarella cheese. I then toast or broil the hearty combination. Upon my first bite, I think of Dad.

3 pounds Yukon potatoes, peeled, cut into 1-inch cubes

salt, to taste

3 tablespoons butter or olive oil

2 tablespoons **Curry Powder**

2 stalks green onions, finely chopped

Add potatoes to a large pot and fill with water until potatoes are covered. Add salt. Bring pot to a boil over high heat, lower heat to a simmer and cook potatoes until tender, when a knife easily pierces through. Drain potatoes in a colander and add back to the pot.

Process potatoes through a ricer or mash with masher. Mix in butter and curry powder until just mixed. Stir in green onions. Serve immediately.

PORK MEATBALLS BANH MI SANDWICHES WITH PICKLED CUCUMBERS AND CARROTS, WITH HOISIN SAUCE

SERVES 4

Bánh mi or banh mi are the Vietnamese words for bread referring to a type of baguette spilt lengthwise as a sandwich. This combination tickles the senses with crunchiness and tenderness combined with salty, sweet and sour. I love having the excuse to venture downtown to Le Fournil to pick up a fresh baguette or, better yet, a black baguette made by owner and baker François Morin with squid ink. This sandwich is perfect to take on a picnic or serve with a bowl of **Cold Carrot Ginger Soup**.

Pork Meatballs
Pickled Cucumbers and Carrots
Homemade Hoisin Sauce
1 fresh baguette
mayonnaise
4 lettuce leaves

Prepare pork meatballs, pickled cucumber and carrots and hoisin sauce according to instructions in this book.

Cut baguette into fourths. Slice each lengthwise just to one edge but not all the way through. Spread some hoisin sauce onto one side of the bread and mayonnaise on the other. Add a lettuce leaf. Put three meatballs into the baguette and stuff in some pickles. Wrap up for a picnic or enjoy immediately.

PORK MEATBALLS

MAKES ABOUT 12 MEATBALLS

This is my modern international take on my mother's dish. These meatballs remind me of the pork cakes she used to make. She would mix the meat with the seasonings, press it into a glass pie dish and place it into a steamer. Steaming meat results in a rather anemic-looking patty, but its lack of prettiness is counterbalanced by its abundance of juice. We ate the meat with the juice spooned over rice. To make these meatballs pretty, I brown them in a skillet and finish them in the oven.

1 pound ground pork

FOR THE SEASONING
1 teaspoon minced ginger
1 stalk green onion, finely chopped
2 cloves garlic, minced
1 tablespoon soy sauce
1 teaspoon dark brown sugar
½ teaspoon **Five-Spice Powder**
1 tablespoon cornstarch

2 tablespoons canola oil

Preheat oven to 375°F. Line a baking sheet with parchment paper and set aside.

In a large bowl, add pork and seasoning ingredients. Combine ingredients until just mixed. Do not overwork. Scoop out 2 tablespoons, form into balls and place onto a plate.

In a large ovenproof skillet, heat oil up over medium-high heat. Add the meatballs to the pan and brown on two sides, about 2 minutes on each side. Do not cook meatballs completely. Place meatballs onto prepared baking sheet in the oven to finish cooking through, about 15 minutes. Cool for 5 minutes before serving.

COOK'S NOTES

The meatballs can be made up the night before. Oftentimes I add everything except the five-spice powder and the cornstarch and keep the pork covered in the refrigerator. Because my husband is not a true fan of five-spice, adding it at the last minute keeps the flavor from being too intense. With the cornstarch, the meat is less "tenderized" yet still soft when it is mixed in at the last minute.

SWEET RICE AND BARLEY COCONUT PUDDING

SERVES 8

As a child, sweet or sticky rice was my ultimate comfort food, with barley running a close second. Both sweet rice and barley are dense and chewy. I find the two make a perfect combination. In this recipe, instead of the more familiar white barley, I use the Timeless Natural Purple Prairie Barley because I love the purple color contrasted against the white rice. As a child, my mother made sticky rice on occasion for a special weekend treat.

If we had any leftovers, I would enjoy it the next day with butter and brown sugar. This pudding is delicious as a dessert or for breakfast with mangos, strawberries, bananas or any seasonal fruit. In the fall, fresh apple or ripe pear slices are great accompaniments. During the holidays, add pomegranate seeds or slices of persimmon.

The butter can be omitted to make the dish vegan. Just add a little bit more coconut milk or substitute with a vegan butter. Vary the amount of milk you use to make the pudding creamier (more) or thicker (less).

1 cup sweet or glutinous rice
½ cup purple barley
2 tablespoons unsalted butter
⅓ cup coconut milk
2 tablespoons dark brown sugar
pinch of salt
1 lime, for zest and juice
½ cup unsweetened coconut flakes, toasted (see Cook's Notes)

Add rice and barley to two separate small bowls (see Cook's Notes). Add water to each bowl to cover grains by half an inch. Cover each bowl and allow to soak at least 4 hours or overnight at room temperature.

Set up steamer (see Cook's Notes). Drain rice and barley and place in steamer basket, mixing the grains as you transfer them. Cook for 45 minutes to 1 hour to desired doneness.

Carefully lift the pan out of the steamer. If there is room for the milk in the pan, just add it directly. If not, transfer the rice and barley to a medium bowl. Add the butter and stir until it is melted. Then add coconut milk, sugar and salt. Scoop pudding into small bowls. Grate lime zest on top of rice. Then slice lime in half and squeeze some juice into each bowl. Garnish with coconut flakes and serve.

COOK'S NOTES

No steamer? Steaming is one of the gentlest ways to cook food. The heat and the moisture of the steam penetrates the food and cooks it. Place a tuna can with both top and bottom removed into the bottom of a wok or soup pot. Make sure the wok or pot has a good lid. If I do not have a can, I will use a large cookie cutter. Find a heatproof plate such as a pie dish or cake pan to fit into the pot, making sure the edge of the pan does not touch the sides of the pot. Make sure you have enough room to safely put the dish into the pot on top of the can or cookie cutter and then safely remove it after the food cooks. The space also allows the steam to rise. Add enough water to the pot to just below the level of the bottom of the dish.

    I use a bamboo steamer to cook the grains. Line the bottom and sides of one of the steaming baskets with cheesecloth or a clean kitchen towel. Add enough water to the pot to below the steamer. Place steamer with rice and barley on top of the pot. Bring water to a boil over high heat. Reduce heat to a simmer, place lid over pot and cook until rice and barley are cooked to your desired softness.

    I recommend Timeless Natural Foods Purple Barley for this dish because it gives it a pretty color. Also, the barley is pump and chewy, giving the pudding a good texture. Because the color is strong, I soak the barley and rice separately, wanting to keep the rice white.

    To toast the coconut, heat coconut in a skillet over medium-low heat until light golden, about 3 to 5 minutes, stirring occasionally. In an oven heated to 325°F, bake until golden, about 10 to 15 minutes. Stir at 5-minute intervals until browned.

FOOD AND DRINK PIONEERS

I have had the honor to talk with culinary pioneers who have elevated the foodscape in our region under the Big Sky. I know they have expanded my palate. From wine, beer and artisan breads to crickets, winemakers, brewers, bakers and farmers are changing the way we eat and drink. They are bringing options to areas where there has been an absence of treasures that are more readily available in larger cities. In most cases, these path builders have had to educate local palates to appreciate their wares.

YELLOWSTONE CELLARS AND WINERY

Clint Peck of Yellowstone Cellars and Winery has made wine in an industrial warehouse on the West End of Billings since 2012. A winemaker who follows the mantra, "Don't say whoa in the middle of a mud hole," he left the cattle business to make wine. His commitment led him to produce a 2010 Malbec that earned him 88 points from *Wine Spectator*. Peck sources his grapes from eastern Washington, driving 750 miles to the Yakima Valley in a truck and trailer to retrieve his grapes. This year, he brought back sixty tons of grapes and will produce about four thousand cases of wine.

DOWNTOWN BILLINGS

In downtown Billings, across from the Northern Hotel, François Morin, owner of Le Fournil bakery, said of baking bread, "I wanted to work with my hands. I wanted to own my own business. I wanted to do something different." After working in the IT business most of his life in France, South Africa and Singapore, he and his wife, Marmee Connell, returned to her hometown. He completed courses at the Bakerz@Work Academy and secured a sourdough starter that was imported to Montana to use in his own baking. Every day except Sundays and Mondays, he bakes about eighty loaves a day in his French oven.

On Montana Avenue, Veronika Baukema focuses on baked products from France, eastern Europe and Russia. Her Uzbekistan origins inspire many of the offerings. In Veronika's Pastry Shop, the French influence shows in her offerings of Almond Croissants, Pain au Chocolat and Chocolate Bouchon. She playfully named her pain aux raisins "Raisin Escargot" (after the French word for snail). Closer to her heritage, Baukema makes traditional fruit- or cheese-filled Russian vatrushka buns, or as they are known in Poland, kolaczki.

Just down the street from the bakery, one encounters MoAv (Montana Avenue) Coffee at the corner of North Twenty-Fifth Street and Montana Avenue in the historic Carlin Hotel, built in 1913. Jeff Hosa, co-owner of MoAv Coffee, confessed, "We always say we are nerds about coffee." From dawn to beyond dusk, this gathering space offers caffeine in the mornings or wine and beer later in the day. MoAv's mission is to "create craft culture through relationship-based innovation. MoAV is a coffee cafe and roastery specializing in coffee profiling, brew methods, craft culture, community and sustainability."

Across the street from MoAv and Veronika's Pastry Shop is Carter's Brewing. In 2007, Michael Uhrich opened the brewery. After graduating with a degree in journalism and unable to find employment, his father-in-law gave him a home brewing kit that ignited his interest in making beer. He apprenticed with George Moncure at Yellowstone Valley Brewing Company for several years, building his fermentation résumé, before opening his own place. Carter's now offers nearly two dozen beers and is part of the Walkable Brewery Trail, featuring seven breweries and one distillery in downtown Billings.

RED LODGE

Red Lodge has become an enclave for talented chefs. Chefs Michael Muirhead of Mas Taco, Chris Lockhart of Prerogative Kitchen and Eric Trager of Carbon Fork have settled under the watch of the Beartooth Mountains. Muirhead received recognitions from the James Beard Foundation as a semifinalist in the Best Chef of the Northwest category in 2016 and 2017. With Alexia and David Leuschen, Lockhart helped start Ox Pasture in 2015 as a launch pad for chefs and their cuisine. Several years later, Lockhart and his wife, Gena Burghoff, along with Danny Mowatt, opened Prerogative Kitchen in the old City Bakery space. Eric Trager began his cooking career in Red Lodge in the original Bridge Creek Back Country and Wine Bar in 1997 to move to new space in 2000. When Bridge Creek closed after fourteen years, Trager moved on to cook at Carbon County Steakhouse and, later, at Piney Dell. These days, he is back in the old Bridge Creek space as owner and chef of his new venture Carbon Fork.

BOZEMAN

In Bozeman, I had the opportunity to visit Cowboy Cricket Farms and Béquet Confections. Under the flight approach at Bozeman Yellowstone Airport in Belgrade, there's

TOP Chef Chris Lockhart (*center*) of Prerogative Kitchen cooks in the Ox Pasture kitchen he started in Red Lodge in 2018.

BOTTOM Chef Michael Muirhead, James Beard Foundation Best Chef semifinalist and owner of Mas Taco in Red Lodge, holds a container of his pickled carrots.

OPPOSITE, TOP Stella Fong interviews Carbon Fork chef Eric Trager at the American Fork Ranch in Two Dot Montana.

OPPOSITE, BOTTOM Judy and Jan Boogman make caramel cookie waffles in their gas-burning stroopwafel oven purchased from Gouda, Holland.

another winged specimen found at Cowboy Cricket Farms. Here high-octane protein products are being produced from *Acheta domesticus*, or the common house cricket, by James and Kathy Rolin, the founders and owners of a business that they advertise "brings bugs to the world in fun and exciting ways."

The company started in 2016 with the Cowboy Chirp Cookie, a chocolate chip cookie made with their own cricket powder. They then ventured into selling snacks of whole crickets in flavors of smoke, cinnamon, wasabi and original. Crickets are 69 percent protein by weight. For example, if one hundred grams of crickets are consumed, sixty-nine grams are protein, while the same amount of chicken supplies thirty-one grams and the same amount of beef has forty-three grams.

From Highway 191, when Ken Siebert and I stepped into Béquet Confections, started by Robin Béquet, we were swaddled in the rich aroma of sugar, butter and cream. In 2001, Béquet made the decision to pursue another career after her job in the medical device industry came to an abrupt end. She decided to turn something that was a hobby into a business. The venture that began in a small space in Four Corners won the "Aisle-by-Aisle" award at the Fancy Food Show in New York in 2005, ranking among the seventeen best products at the show. Since then, she has won numerous awards for her confections. These days, there are thirteen different flavors, from butterscotch to green apple.

Also, in Bozeman I need to give a shout-out to Claudia Krevat of Claudia's Mesa in Bozeman. This maven of legumes educates home cooks and food service workers in Montana about lentils through her community dinners and cooking classes. Her work with Timeless Seeds is changing the way we see and eat lentils and chickpeas under the Big Sky.

With equally dynamic flavors, Andleeb Dawood, owner of Saffron Table with her chef, Daniel Parris, brought food from Dawood's childhood in Pakistan to be presented in the Montana way by the Choteau native.

BILLINGS STRONGHOLDS

Finally, I would be remiss if I did not mention Caramel Cookie Waffles and Brockel's Chocolates in Billings. Jan and Judy Boogman have been making stroopwafels on Seventeenth Street since 1981, while Patti and Gary Brockel, along with daughters Jaci and Jodi and granddaughter Savannah, have been making chocolates since 1979. To this day, Jan and Judy Boogman still hand-make the caramel cookie waffles in the same massive stroopwafel oven they purchased from Gouda, Holland, when they started the business.

TOP François and Marmee Morin, owners of Le Fournil, bake up fresh loaves of French bread in downtown Billings.

BOTTOM In Bozeman, Saffron Table's owner Andleeb Dawood from Pakistan and Chef Daniel Parris from Choteau, Montana, exemplify the joining of foreign flavors with local talent.

TOP Claudia Krevat of Claudia's Mesa in Bozeman educates cooks about lentils and other legumes from Montana.

BOTTOM Robin Béquet, founder of Béquet Confections, started her caramel business in Bozeman in 2001.

The Brockels still sell apples coated with the caramel recipe handed down to them from Wilcoxson's Ice Cream Company, the previous owner.

Both businesses have remained in their original location. Jan admitted that he never expanded the business because he enjoyed having customer contact. He was not interested in running a cookie factory, but he may have summarized the sentiments of both his business and Brockel's when he said, "We really feel grounded in this community, and I feel like we have a good handle on the quality and service so we can give customers a good value."

My gratitude to the producers and growers who create bounty for the community to celebrate under the Big Sky.

PART II
RIVERS AND LAKES

Throughout Montana, rivers and lakes abound. The Continental Divide of the Rocky Mountains extends north and south on the western part of the state, separating west-sloping and east-sloping drainages. The west artery extends to the Pacific Ocean, whereas the other flows to the Atlantic. A third drainage from Glacier National Park moves water to Canada. In northeastern Montana, at the Fork Peck Reservoir, Pacific salmon (Chinook) were planted in the 1980s. The rivers and alpine lakes are abundant with wild trout across the state. The environment near these waters provides the optimal place for bounty such as morels and asparagus. The famous Flathead Lake provides the perfect microclimate for cherries and peaches to flourish. In this section, the recipes from and near these waters are brought to the table.

ASPARAGUS, RADISH AND CHERRY SALAD

SERVES 4 TO 8

The combination of asparagus, radishes and cherries is surprising. Rarely do we think of eating asparagus raw, but its taste combines the best of green beans and broccoli in one slender shoot. A bunch of radishes often sits in my refrigerator because they are easy to throw on a cheese plate with a small bowl of salt if you get unexpected guests. They are pretty with their rosettes and long stems while popping with spice and zest.

Here under the Big Sky, Flathead Lake cherries are the crown jewels of summer. These fleshy, crimson-colored fruits are usually subtly sweet and are a great addition to this salad. I always buy more cherries than I need to pit and freeze for enjoyment beyond summer.

FOR THE DRESSING

⅓ cup extra virgin olive oil

⅓ cup white wine vinegar

2 tablespoons honey

salt, to taste

fresh ground black pepper, to taste

1 pound asparagus, cut diagonally into 1-inch slices

6 radishes, cut into wedges

1 cup cherries, halved, pits removed

1 small shallot, halved lengthwise, thinly sliced

In a small bowl, whisk together dressing ingredients. Set aside. In a large bowl, toss asparagus, radishes, cherries and shallot with dressing. Serve immediately.

MOREL CROSTINI

SERVES 4 TO 6

My husband's mantra is "Keep it simple." He is a good balance for me because I tend to make things more complicated than they need to be. Morels are special, so simple is superior. The sautéed mushrooms without the baguette would go perfectly with the **Chive Dutch Baby** *served at brunch or dinner with the* **Butter Lettuce Salad**.

During the off season, I keep a bag of dried morels in my pantry, which work perfectly in this dish. In season, usually in the month of May, go with what is freshly available harvested from your own hunt, purchased from the Missoula Farmers' Market or gifted to you from a dear friend.

1 baguette, thinly sliced

⅓ cup extra virgin olive oil

2 tablespoons unsalted butter

6 ounces fresh morels, cleaned and sliced lengthwise

1 tablespoon soy sauce

3 stalks green onions, diagonally sliced

salt, to taste

fresh ground black pepper, to taste

1 teaspoon lemon juice

2 sprigs Italian flat leaf parsley, leaves removed, stems discarded

Heat oven to 350°F. Brush both sides of baguette slices with olive oil. Place on baking sheet and bake until bread is toasted, about 10 to 15 minutes. Place pieces on a platter and set aside.

In a large skillet, melt butter over medium-high heat. Add the morels and sauté until morels are tender, about 5 minutes. Add soy sauce and cook for 1 minute, letting mushrooms absorb the sauce. Add green onions and cook for 1 minute. Season with salt and pepper to taste. Squeeze lemon juice on top of mushrooms.

Pour mushrooms into a serving bowl and garnish with parsley. Place bowl on top of the platter with toasted baguette slices. Enjoy with spoonfuls of mushrooms on top of toast.

COOK'S NOTE

If using fresh mushrooms, soak mushrooms quickly in cold water. Then drain in a strainer to rid of any sand or dirt and any excess water. Set aside. In a pot, boil water for reheating pasta and then keep warm until ready to use.

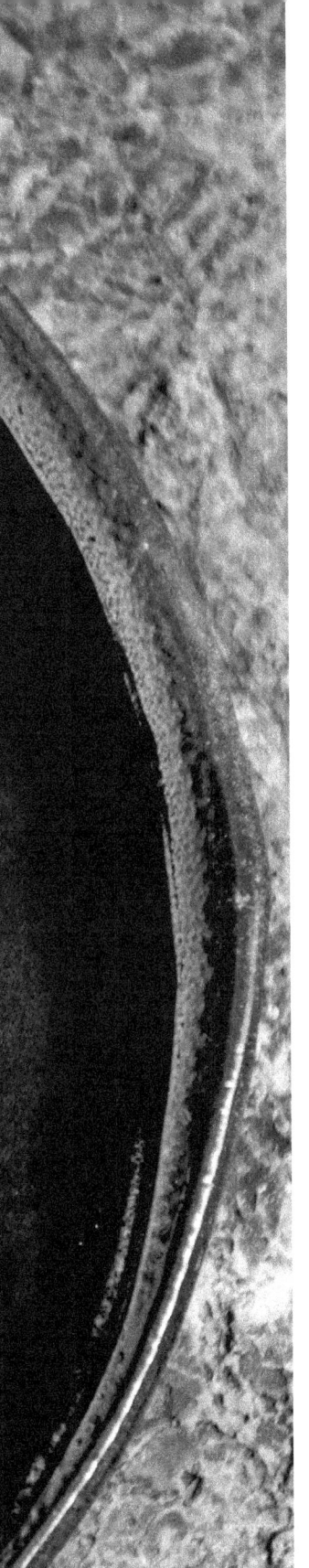

SMASHED POTATOES WITH SMOKED TROUT

SERVES 4 TO 6

Smashed potatoes can go with everything and eaten at all meals. For breakfast, this dish is delicious with poached eggs or **Chive Dutch Baby** *and, at lunch, served as a side to a sandwich. For dinner, serve this with* **Butter Lettuce Salad** *for a light meal, but this is best as an appetizer for a crowd. Smoked trout is one of my favorite kinds of smoked fish. It is less fishy in taste than salmon and less dense in texture.*

1½ pounds small Yukon potatoes, scrubbed, peel on

2 tablespoons extra virgin olive oil

4 cloves garlic, minced

4 sprigs fresh dill plus 2 sprigs, about 4 inches long

salt, to taste

fresh ground black pepper, to taste

8 ounces smoked trout, skins discarded, meat flaked into large chunks

FOR THE GARNISH

⅓ cup sour cream

¼ cup chopped chives

dill sprigs

Heat oven to 425°F. Line a baking sheet with parchment paper. Set aside.

Add potatoes to a medium pot. Add water to about 1 inch above the surface of the potatoes. Add salt to taste. Bring to a boil. Lower heat and simmer for 12 to 15 minutes or until potatoes are tender. Drain.

In a large bowl, add warm potatoes and toss with oil and garlic. Spread potatoes over prepared baking sheet. With a fork, smash potatoes to a flat patty, about half an inch thick. Break leaves off of 4 dill sprigs and sprinkle on top of potatoes. Sprinkle salt to taste and add a generous grind of fresh ground black pepper. Bake until potatoes are browned and crisp, about 35 to 45 minutes. Transfer potatoes to a platter. Scatter smoked trout on top of potatoes. Garnish with sour cream and chives. Coarsely break dill sprigs on top. Serve immediately.

CEDAR PLANKED SALMON WITH PRESERVED LEMON, BLACK BEAN AND CHIVE BUTTER

SERVES 2

One of the best ways to grill salmon is on a cedar plank. The plank, together with the compound butter and a thermometer, guarantees succulent salmon. Chinook, also known as "king salmon," are found in northeastern Montana, where they are stocked in the Fort Peck Reservoir. If you are not fortunate enough to hook your own salmon, Seafoods of the World in Billings has been my dependable resource for fish.

1 cedar plank (6x14 inches)

FOR COMPOUND BUTTER

½ cup butter

2 cloves garlic

2 tablespoons salt fermented black beans, rinsed and drained

2 teaspoons preserved lemons

¼ cup chopped chives

juice of one lemon

2 salmon fillets, skin on, about 1½ pounds

Soak cedar plank in water for 2 hours, drain. In a food processor bowl, add ingredients for compound butter. Pulse until all ingredients are finely minced. Transfer mixture to a small bowl and set aside.

Remove any bones from salmon if necessary. Rinse salmon under cold running water and pat dry with paper towels.

Lay salmon skin-side down on the cedar plank and carefully spread the butter over the top.

Heat grill to medium high. Set plank in the center of the hot grate, away from direct heat. Cover the grill and cook about 20 to 30 minutes, until internal temperature just reaches 135°F. Transfer the salmon and plank to a platter and serve from the plank.

JAMES HONAKER'S MOREL MUSHROOM SHERRY THYME CREAM SAUCE

SERVES 2 OR 4 AS AN APPETIZER

After Trevor McFarren took me morel mushroom hunting in Billings, I took the bounty to Bistro Enzo, where Executive Chef James Honaker talked us through making a pasta dish for Flavors Under the Big Sky. *I have modified this recipe to use generic dry sherry instead of amontillado, which is a variety characterized by being darker than fino, the lightest of sherries. I then opted for a rigatoni pasta, as the crevices trap and hold the delectable sauce more tightly than Honaker's recommended angel hair pasta.*

- 4 ounces dried morel mushrooms
- 3 tablespoons extra virgin olive oil
- 1 small red onion, thinly sliced
- 2 cloves garlic, minced
- ½ teaspoon salt or to taste
- 4 to 6 stalks of asparagus, trimmed, sliced on a diagonal
- 4 sprigs of fresh thyme, leaves removed
- 2 tablespoons dry sherry
- ¼ cup white wine
- 1 teaspoon salt or to taste
- 1 tablespoon lemon zest, finely grated
- ⅓ cup veal or chicken stock
- ½ cup heavy cream
- 8 ounces rigatoni pasta, cooked
- ¼ pound Parmigiano-Reggiano, grated

Soak morel mushrooms in hot water for 30 minutes. Drain and discard (or save soaking liquid making sure to strain out any sand or dirt for a broth or for use in a sauce; keep in refrigerator or freezer until use). Trim morels if necessary and then cut in half lengthwise. Set aside.

Heat oil in sauté pan over medium-high heat, add onion and garlic and cook until fragrant, about 2 minutes. Sprinkle in salt. Add asparagus and cook for 1 minute. Add thyme, sherry and white wine. Cook for 2 minutes. Add mushrooms and cook for 5 to 6 minutes, lowering heat to a simmer. Add salt, to taste. Stir in lemon zest and add stock. Simmer for 1 minute and then add the cream. Simmer until sauce thickens to the consistency of syrup, about 5 to 10 minutes.

Turn water back up to boiling. Quickly heat pasta in the water, drain thoroughly. Toss with sauce in pan. Divide evenly onto plates and serve with freshly shaved Parmigiano-Reggiano cheese.

ASPARAGUS TORTILLA

SERVES 4

For breakfast or brunch, I depend on this recipe. It can be made in stages, plus it is versatile. The potatoes can be cooked beforehand. In fact, use up other kinds of cooked potatoes if you have them on hand. The potatoes give this egg dish a solid base. Substitute the cheese and the asparagus with other options of cheese types and vegetables.

This tortilla is my Spanish version of the American omelet or Italian frittata, but the difference is the tortilla is traditionally made with eggs and potatoes. In Spain, the tortilla is served as an appetizer at room temperature. If you want to serve this at a cocktail gathering, you can cut it up in cubes and stick a toothpick into each piece.

- 1 pound medium Yukon potatoes
- 8 eggs
- 1 tablespoon extra virgin olive oil or unsalted butter
- salt, to taste
- fresh ground black pepper, to taste
- ½ cup grated Manchego
- ½ pound asparagus
- 1 stalk green onion, thinly sliced
- ⅓ cup chopped Italian parsley
- ½ cup sour cream

Place potatoes in a saucepan filled with water to about 1 inch above the potatoes. Bring to a boil and reduce to a simmer. Cover pot and cook for 20 to 30 minutes or until tender in the center when pierced with a knife. Drain potatoes and allow to cool to room temperature. Peel the potatoes if desired. Otherwise, slice them into ¼-inch-thick slices.

Heat broiler to high.

Break eggs into a bowl and whisk until mixture is frothy and there are no longer streaks of white or yellow. Set aside.

Heat oil in a 12-inch nonstick pan over medium heat. Layer potatoes onto the bottom of the pan. Season with salt and pepper to taste. Cook for 1 minute. Pour in eggs and cook for another minute. Sprinkle cheese evenly over the eggs. Lay the asparagus spears on top of the cheese. Cook on stove top for 5 to 10 minutes until eggs are set on the sides and more than midway through. Sprinkle on green onion and parsley. Place pan under the broiler until top is barely set and slightly browned but not overcooked. Slide tortilla onto a serving dish. Cut into wedges. Serve immediately or at room temperature with some sour cream.

COOK'S NOTES

Short on time? Make this tortilla the night before. Wrap it in foil and then reheat it just before service at 325°F for 20 to 25 minutes until it is warmed through. Place it on a serving dish and slice it into wedges.

ROASTED ASPARAGUS

SERVES 4

*Roasting is one of the best ways to enjoy the bountiful spring asparagus. At the beginning of the week, I roast a few pounds to keep in the refrigerator to add to salads or to an **Asparagus Tortilla**—or just to snack on. This is another treat that can be added to a cheese plate if someone drops by.*

1 pound asparagus
1 tablespoon extra virgin olive oil
generous pinch of salt

Trim bottoms of asparagus and, with a vegetable peeler, shave off any tough sides near the bottom of the stalk. In a large bowl, toss asparagus with olive oil and salt. Set aside.

Heat grill to medium high. Throw spears on top of grill and cook long enough to get grill marks, about 2 to 4 minutes on each side.

COOK'S NOTES

Alternatively, place the asparagus on a baking sheet and cook 4 inches under the broiler until the spears brown, about 2 to 4 minutes. I usually just cook one side, wanting to keep the asparagus on the al dente side.

SPARKLING CHERRY SANGRIA

SERVES 8

Sangria is one of the best ways to enjoy the cherries of the season. Early on, sour cherries are the first to be harvested. Later, Bing cherries ripen and can go into this spirited drink. The cherries marinate in the wine and spirits overnight, becoming more flavorful and intense. Using rosé wine lets the cherries shine and not be masked by a deep red wine. I use Yellowstone Cellars and Winery's Syrah-based rosé. The aromas of raspberries, strawberries and pomegranate and the notes of lilac and violets make the perfect backdrop for this sangria. This drink sings summer and is ideal for sipping outside in the backyard or on the balcony when it is hot, or as a reminder of warmer temperatures when winter reigns. Salud!

FOR SUGAR SYRUP
½ cup sugar
½ cup water

2 cups cherries, pitted
1 bottle dry rosé wine
½ cup brandy
¼ cup gin
¼ cup Cherry Heering or other cherry liqueur
1 liter club soda, chilled
whole cherries with stems, for garnish
mint and thyme sprigs, for garnish

In a small saucepan, bring sugar and water to a simmer, cooking until sugar dissolves. Remove from heat and allow sugar syrup to cool.

Into a pitcher, add syrup, cherries, rosé, brandy, gin and cherry liqueur. Chill in refrigerator overnight.

Just before serving, add club soda. Pour into glasses filled with ice. Garnish with cherry and sprigs of mint and thyme.

PAVLOVA ROULADE WITH SOUR CHERRY SAUCE AND TOASTED ALMONDS

SERVES 8

Dreamy. This dessert is heavenly—rich and so easy to eat. The recipe came to life because we have two sour cherry trees in our backyard. This year, we picked about 30 quarts of cherries. Pie is the obvious recipe for these amazing cherries, but they are so lovely served in a roulade.

The sauce in this recipe can be used for ice cream or cake for dessert, but it is also delectable slathered on a piece of toast or on top of yogurt for breakfast. The sauce is also delicious with grilled pork.

The pavlova can get crumbly, especially when you start rolling it. Just gather the pieces and throw them back on top of the roll as a crumble. The lovely natural defects can be covered up later with cream and a dusting of confectioners' sugar.

⅓ cup raw almond slices

extra confectioners' sugar for rolling and dusting

FOR THE SAUCE

6 tablespoons sugar

pinch of salt

¼ cup water plus 1 tablespoon, divided

2 cups sour cherries, stems removed, pitted

2 teaspoons cornstarch

FOR THE PAVLOVA

4 egg whites

1¼ cups sugar

1 teaspoon cornstarch

1 teaspoon almond extract

½ teaspoon vanilla extract

1 teaspoon white vinegar

FOR THE CREAM

1½ cups heavy cream

1 tablespoon confectioners' sugar

½ cup mascarpone

1 teaspoon almond extract

Heat oven to 325°F. Spread almonds in a single layer on a baking sheet. Bake for 4 to 5 minutes, being sure almonds do not burn by checking every minute until lightly browned. Set aside.

Line the bottom and sides of a 9x13-inch baking pan with parchment paper. Let the parchment paper rise about 1-inch above the sides of the pan. Set aside.

FOR THE SAUCE

Add sugar, salt and ¼ cup water to a saucepan. Bring to a boil and cook until sugar and salt are dissolved. Add cherries and bring back to a boil. Lower heat and simmer for 2 minutes. In a small bowl, dissolve cornstarch in 1 tablespoon water. Whisk in cornstarch and cook until thickened, about 1 minute. Set aside and cool to room temperature.

FOR THE PAVLOVA

In a large bowl, beat the egg whites with an electric mixer until foamy. Add the sugar in a slow, steady stream. Continue beating until a firm, glossy meringue forms. Sift cornstarch on top of the egg white mixture. With a metal spoon, fold in extracts and vinegar. Spread meringue into prepared pan, making sure the top is even.

Bake for 25 minutes or until a light crust forms and top starts to brown. Allow pavlova to cool in the pan.

FOR THE CREAM

Beat heavy cream with an electric mixer until soft peaks form. Add sugar and beat for 1 minute. Beat in mascarpone and almond extract until cream just holds its shape, about 3 minutes. (Do not overmix.) Cover and refrigerate.

Unmold the cooled meringue onto a kitchen towel dusted with 2 tablespoons of confectioners' sugar. Carefully pull off the lining parchment paper. Reserve about ½ cup cream mixture while spreading the rest on top of the underside of the pavlova, leaving a small border around the edge. Scoop about 1 cup of cherries with as little sauce as possible onto cream.

Using the towel, starting on the long edge, roll up meringue into a log. Carefully place the log on a platter. Dollop cream on top of meringue and refrigerate for at least 30 minutes.

When ready to serve, drizzle sauce on top of meringue. Scatter almonds over the top finishing with a dusting of confectioners' sugar.

> **COOK'S NOTES**
>
> No sour cherries? Use Bing cherries or Rainer cherries, using less sugar and a squeeze of lemon juice. Otherwise, blackberries or peaches work in this recipe too. You can use fresh fruit such as sliced strawberries. During the holidays, when persimmons or pomegranates are available, they can be used fresh in this dessert.

PRAIRIE SURPRISE COWBOY COOKIES

MAKES 3 TO 3½ DOZEN COOKIES

This cookie can fuel a cowboy, athlete or anyone needing energy to get through a physical challenge. The ingredients that inspired this cookie recipe came from my visit to Cowboy Cricket Farms in Belgrade and from a Flavor Moments with Brockel's Chocolates in Billings. With protein, fat, carbohydrates and caffeine, not to mention the extra protein provided by roasted crickets, these cookies are good to have in a saddlebag or backpack. A cricket is 65 percent protein and contains additional nutrients, such as B12, Omega-3s, Omega-6s and more. This cookie is perfect for dipping into a cup of coffee fancied with chocolate milk.

3 cups all-purpose flour
1 tablespoon baking powder
2 teaspoons baking soda
1 teaspoon ground cinnamon
1 teaspoon salt
1 cup (2 sticks) butter, at room temperature
½ cup peanut butter
1½ cups sugar
1 cup packed dark brown sugar
3 eggs
2 tablespoons vanilla
3 cups old-fashioned rolled oats
2 cups chopped walnuts
2 cups semisweet chocolate chips
1 cup chocolate covered espresso beans, coarsely crushed
½ cup dry roasted crickets, coarsely chopped

Heat oven to 350°F. Line baking sheets with parchment paper. Set aside.

In a medium bowl, mix together flour, baking powder, baking soda, cinnamon and salt.

In a large bowl, with an electric mixer, beat butter and peanut butter until creamy and smooth. Gradually beat in sugars and mix thoroughly.

Beat in eggs one at a time. Mix in vanilla.

Stir in flour mixture until just combined. Stir in oats, walnuts, chocolate chips, espresso beans and crickets.

For each cookie, drop about ¼ cup dough onto prepared baking sheets, spacing about 3 inches apart. Bake for 15 to 20 minutes, until edges are lightly browned. Let cookies cool for about 5 minutes to remove to cool on rack.

JAMES HONAKER AND TREVOR MCFARREN: THE CHEF AND THE MOREL HUNTER

Executive Chef James Honaker has been keeping the beat at Bistro Enzo for more than twenty years. Even though he has been nominated three times by the James Beard Foundation as a semifinalist for Best Chef in the Northwest, he still shies away from the public eye. The kitchen is where he is most comfortable, where he retreats after an occasional obligatory appearance in the dining room.

For me, it was Honaker's shyness, grounded with humbleness, that endeared me to him. He never filled the airwaves with braggadocio, but instead harbored touches of self-doubt when, in reality, he just cooked, and cooked very well.

Food is Honaker's passion. Even though he ventured to New York in the 1970s to pursue a career in jazz drumming, he ended up taking courses at Peter Kump's New York Cooking School and eventually received training at the New York Restaurant School. Then fate brought him to cook at Windows of the World, where he gained wine knowledge with innovator Raymond Wellington.

On the other culinary coast, Honaker became a guest chef at Beringer's Winery and then cooked at Gerard's Brasserie in San Francisco, where he met up with Laurent Zirotti and Patricia Rolland. While Zirotti and Rolland returned to France, Honaker ventured to New York to attend film school on a scholarship that required him to work if he was to survive. Fortuitously, in 1986 he ran into Chef Eric Ripert as he was opening Le Bernardin. The Paris-based, two-Michelin-star restaurant served only seafood, and owners Maguy and Gilbert Le Coze wanted to open a sister establishment in New York.

When Honaker, Zirotti and Rolland reunited on Flathead Lake on a summer retreat, they decided to join forces in Billings to open La Toque. The intimate, authentic French restaurant lasted only two years, for it was ahead of its time. To this day, this is still one restaurant many bring up as a memorable spot from Billings's past.

Honaker returned to New York to work at Le Boule, obtaining bread baking skills, while Zirotti took on the deputy general manager position at the Hotel Majestic on the French Riviera in Cannes. Then, in November 1998, Honaker, Zirotti and the now Mrs. Zirotti, Patricia, opened Enzo Mediterranean Bistro in a red terra cotta–tiled, yellow stucco building on the west end of Billings, at the edge of a shopping center and right next to a fast-food establishment. The 140-seat restaurant took on the name of the Zirottis' oldest son. Both men shared the cooking, with Zirotti taking on front of the house duties on occasion. Guests anticipated greetings from both Patricia and Laurent, while women diners always looked forward to Laurent's multiple-kiss greetings.

TOP Chef James Honaker has been at the helm of the Bistro Enzo kitchen in Billings for more than twenty years.

BOTTOM Trevor McFarren introduced me to a bountiful hunt for the illusive morel mushroom.

The Zirottis left Billings to open their own French restaurant in Post Falls, Idaho, called Fleur de Sel in 2008. Honaker renamed his restaurant Bistro Enzo and, for some time, continued to serve American, French, Italian and Asian-inspired cuisine. Recently, he revised his menu to have a more French Mediterranean focus, with salads and soups now served á la carte.

Two years ago, in the spring, after eating a dish with pasta and morel mushrooms at the restaurant, I asked Honaker if he would reveal his supplier for these elusive mushrooms. Without hesitancy, he said he would contact him to ask if he would talk to me. Within a day, I received a phone number for Trevor McFarren. Although I had generous friends—such as Marilyn and Wiley Bland, Margit Thorndal and Ginnie Pueringer—who took me on hikes to their secret sources or invited me along to explore, I could not believe that someone who supplied a restaurant was willing to actually show me how to hunt for morels.

Over the years, I still smile at those people who told me about the garbage bag full of bounty they managed to secure. They exuded enthusiasm about their discovery, but then something would suddenly stop them from divulging everything, as though something had grabbed them and told them to shut up.

Until I saw a man sitting on the tailgate of his truck and donning a pair of waders in the Burger King parking lot, I believed that McFarren would have second thoughts. After I put on my waders to protect against ticks, I followed him in my car to Riverfront Park.

At this point, I had released one layer of my anxieties, since McFarren did show up, but this was one of my first outings using my own recorder. I would have to not only walk, talk and record but also hunt. After getting out of the car, we hiked on a dirt path with McFarren all the while talking, scanning the edges of the path we were on. Every now and then, we headed into patches under the trees, where old leaves rested, and into small patches where logs had fallen. We waded through a few coulees and even combed a grassy patch. Under foliage cover, dappled light tricked us into seeing images that were not there.

About fifteen minutes into our walk, I spotted the first morel mushroom in a grove of trees atop slightly wet, matted dried leaves. I gasped and said, "Look, over there." In a split second, a half dozen conical-shaped objects, about an inch or two tall, appeared. As I looked around, I focused on several more, as though a light turned on.

McFarren complimented me on the find. He was truly happy for me. I was grateful for his direction and helping me to pay attention and focus on the prize. He pulled out a plastic bag from his pocket and walked over to the morel that stood tallest in the sunlight. He carefully broke the mushroom at the base with his fingers, as he wanted to leave a stem for possible regeneration.

For the next half hour or so, we continued to find morels. I came to believe in magic, that rabbits could be pulled out of hats and that pennies lived behind my ears. Once we saw one mushroom, McFarren squatted down ever so slightly and, with his eyes, swept a path to it. He then scanned the area near that beacon, starting close and then spreading slowly beyond. He had successfully hunted morels on many occasions.

McFarren was delighted with each discovery. With each mushroom, he was gentle and made sure to leave the base behind. We stopped after securing about a pound of bounty. McFarren would have kept hunting, but I felt as though I had overstayed my welcome. I was a guest in his house, and although I appreciated his hospitality, I felt it was time for me to go.

Before I ended the interview, he insisted on taking me to his hiding place by the river, where he and his fellow foragers had built a bench to watch the river flow by.

That afternoon, Ken Siebert, my husband and I went to Bistro Enzo with the collected bounty. Ken recorded as I talked to Chef Honaker and Joe took pictures. The man who was often an apparition in the dining room when diners were present transformed into a talkative and informative teacher. In the kitchen, this Clark Kent became Superman.

In this show, Chef Honaker shared with the listeners how to make a Morel Mushroom Sherry Cream Sauce with pasta. He quickly rinsed the morels in cold water and then cut each one in half, looking for a hollow interior, since false morels are solid and can be odiferous. A whole shallot quickly became thin slices, while his minced garlic appeared almost microscopic, as Honaker worked his knife.

While cooking, Honaker waited for the evolution of flavors from the shallots and garlic. He allowed flavors to meld and cream to thicken. When everything was in place, he added the mushrooms, letting them bathe in the simmer of the sauce. The beauty of the morel is that it has hollow cells, which provide room for sauces and flavors to seep in.

Honaker stressed the importance of getting basic cooking skills and, even more, following the rules of good cooking. "Learn your craft," he stressed, for "creativity is a sin. Learning the basics will provide good grounding for cooking."

While the Billings community is glad that Chef Honaker is playing his drums on occasion on Sunday nights at Walkers Grill, we are even happier that at Bistro Enzo, he is still playing with the right timing. As for Trevor McFarren, his timing was also right in showing me where I could find the illusive morel mushroom.

PART III
MOUNTAINS

With the name "Montana" meaning mountain in the Spanish language, it is no wonder that the world knows this state for its highest geological features. There are at least one hundred ranges and subranges in the fourth-largest state, mostly on the west side. The mountains are where elk bugle, huckleberries sweeten the flora and roses beautify the landscape.

PAN SEARED ELK FAJITAS FOR TACOS

SERVES 4 TO 6

The secret to the success of elk fajitas is cooking the meat on a hot pan to quickly sear the meat. This gives the meat color and produces good caramelized flavors. This is especially important because elk does not have much fat. Also, the addition of cornstarch keeps the meat tender.

*My meat was given to me from my friend Kim Hauptman. Her husband, Tom, is the true example of a Montana hunter in his dedication and determination, getting out every season to secure meat for his family. The Hauptmans gave me a sample of elk to cook when we first moved here. I stir-fried the meat with a similar recipe for **Pheasant Stir-Fry with Black Bean Sauce** and found it delicious.*

I discovered that in September and October, bright blinding orange became the color I would see people wear. At gatherings, conversations focused on securing tags and where elk had been spotted to fill freezers with bounty. Yes, Stella, I have a feeling we're not in San Diego anymore.

1½ to 2 pounds elk steak, thinly sliced

FOR THE MARINADE

2 tablespoons extra virgin olive oil

¼ cup soy sauce

1 tablespoon lime juice

4 cloves garlic, minced

FOR THE SEASONING

1 tablespoon cornstarch

1 tablespoon ground cumin

2 teaspoons smoked paprika

½ teaspoon ground coriander

1 teaspoon salt

2 tablespoons plus 2 tablespoons canola or vegetable oil, divided, plus extra if necessary

In a medium bowl, mix elk with marinade ingredients. Marinate in refrigerator for at least 1 hour or overnight.

Mix in seasoning ingredients with marinated meat. Let sit at room temperature for 30 minutes.

Heat oil in wok or skillet over medium-high heat. Break meat apart and add just enough to pan to cover the bottom, making sure pieces do not touch. (See Cook's Notes.) Sear on one side for 1 to 2 minutes or until browned. Turn and brown the other side, 1 to 2 minutes. Scoop out of pan and set aside on a plate while you finish cooking all of the meat, repeating with heating the oil and searing the meat. Serve immediately with serving suggestions below for tacos.

COOK'S NOTES

It is important that the pan is hot with the oil swirling and smoking slightly. Unsticking the meat and making sure that individual pieces hit the pan are important for getting the right browning. Adding the meat in a clump will steam the meat, and although you will get tender results, you won't have the nice caramelized color and flavor.

FOR SERVING

12 to 14 taco-size flour or corn tortillas

Roasted Tomatillo Salsa

sour cream

hot sauce

lime wedges

cilantro

Cotija cheese

chopped avocados

ELK KIELBASA WITH POMEGRANATE

SERVES 4 TO 6

Pomegranate seeds are the gems of fall. They bring color and brightness to a dish. With both elk and pomegranate showcasing as bounty toward the end of the year, they are the perfect pairing. Kielbasa, a sausage originating from Poland, exudes garlicky goodness, pairing well with the refreshing pomegranate and lime. I like serving this dish with Chinese soup spoons so you can scoop up all the deliciousness. When I cannot get wild game, my main source is 4th Avenue Meat Market in downtown Billings.

FOR THE SAUCE

¼ cup pomegranate molasses
¼ cup extra virgin olive oil
2 tablespoons honey
1 tablespoon soy sauce
1 tablespoon ketchup
1 teaspoon Dijon mustard
salt, to taste
fresh ground black pepper, to taste

1 pound elk kielbasa, cut into ½- to 1-inch slices
1 cup pomegranate seeds
⅓ cup minced flat-leaf parsley
1 small lime, for zest and juice
salt, to taste
fresh ground black pepper, to taste

In a large bowl, mix together the sauce ingredients. Toss in sausage to coat with the sauce. Cover and let sit in refrigerator for at least an hour and up to overnight.

Heat oven to 350°F.

In a medium bowl, combine pomegranate seeds, parsley, zest, juice and salt and pepper to taste. Set aside.

Spray a baking dish with cooking oil spray. Scoop in sausage mixture and bake for 30 minutes. Remove from oven and let meat sit for about 5 minutes. Stir in pomegranate mixture. Serve immediately.

COOK'S NOTES

No pomegranate molasses? Substitute balsamic vinegar with a touch of sugar, tamarind paste with some honey or cranberry juice with some molasses. No pomegranate seeds? Blueberries and seedless red grapes are good substitutes. Be sure to quarter the grapes for more bite-size samples.

PORK TENDERLOIN WITH HUCKLEBERRY HOISIN GINGER GLAZE

SERVES 6 TO 8

*This dish brings together my two worlds of flavors: China and Montana. The secret to tender pork is brining, but if you are tight on time, skip the step. Just sprinkle the tenderloin with salt and pepper and grill. The glaze of the **Homemade Hoisin Sauce** with huckleberry preserves is the delicious finishing touch. Slice the tenderloin and serve with extra sauce with **Mandarin Pancakes**.*

FOR THE BRINE

2 cups warm water
¼ cup salt
2 tablespoons red wine vinegar
2 tablespoons brown sugar
1 teaspoon red pepper flakes
1 cup ice
2 pork tenderloins, about 1 to 1¼ pounds each, trimmed

FOR THE SAUCE

1 tablespoon unsalted butter
2 cloves garlic, minced
2 teaspoons minced ginger
½ teaspoon red pepper flakes
½ cup huckleberry preserves
¼ cup **Homemade Hoisin Sauce**
2 tablespoons red wine vinegar
salt, to taste
fresh ground black pepper, to taste

1 tablespoon extra virgin olive oil
salt, to taste
fresh ground black pepper, to taste

Combine water, salt, vinegar, sugar and pepper flakes in a medium pot over high heat. Bring to just a boil, stirring to dissolve salt. Let stand for 10 minutes.

Add ice to a medium bowl. Pour brine over ice and stir until ice melts. Place tenderloins in a large plastic bag and pour brine over pork. Seal and refrigerate for 8 hours or overnight.

In a medium saucepan, melt butter over medium-high heat. Add garlic and ginger and cook for 2 minutes or until garlic softens. Stir in pepper flakes, huckleberry preserves, hoisin sauce, vinegar and salt and pepper, to taste. Keep sauce warm.

Remove pork from bag and pat dry with paper towel. Rub with olive oil and salt and pepper, to taste.

Heat grill to medium high. Place the tenderloin on the grill. Cover and cook until grill marks form, about 5 to 7 minutes. Flip pork and cook for another 5 to 7 minutes to mark the meat. Then cook until the internal temperature reaches 140°F to 145°F, about another 10 minutes of cooking. Lightly brush meat with sauce and cook for another minute on each side.

Remove the tenderloin from the grill to a cutting board. Tent loosely with aluminum foil and allow to rest for 10 minutes for meat to finish cooking and the juices to redistribute.

Slice meat and serve with warm sauce.

MANDARIN PANCAKES

MAKES ABOUT 20 PANCAKES

This recipe was inspired by my mentor, Lily Loh, who provided me recipes for much of the food I grew up with. Since my father cooked by memory, I do not recall seeing him use written instructions for his cooking. Everything was made with all his senses. He just knew how food should be when it came together.

Before Lily retired from teaching Chinese cooking classes, she took me under her wing. We collaborated on several projects, including an article on stir-fried dishes for Cooking Light *magazine.*

This recipe is one that I keep around, as the pancakes can be used as wraps for just about anything. They are the Chinese tortillas or naan, packaging food for easy eating. These pancakes, with **Pork Tenderloin with Huckleberry Hoisin Ginger Glaze***, are usually a crowd favorite in our house.*

2 cups all-purpose flour plus extra flour for dusting
¾ cup boiling water
about ½ cup sesame oil

Add flour to a mixing bowl and pour in boiling water. Using a spatula, bring flour and water together, scraping the sides of the bowl. Turn dough onto a flat, lightly floured work surface and knead until smooth and elastic. Cover with a towel and let sit for 15 minutes.

Roll dough into a long log on lightly floured surface. With a knife, cut dough into about 20 pieces of equal size. Gently roll pieces into a ball. Flatten ball dough to about ¼-inch-thick disk. Brush sesame oil onto the surface of disk. Gently press another disk on top. On a lightly floured surface, roll both pieces of dough into an 8-inch round.

Heat a skillet over medium heat. Add the double pancake and cook for about 1 minute on each side until the pancake turns white and has a few spots. Remove from the pan. Gently separate the two pancakes, peeling one pancake from the other. Stack pancakes on top of each other and cover with a towel.

COOK'S NOTES

These pancakes are best eaten right away. To reheat, wrap pancakes in aluminum foil and heat in a 300°F oven for about 10 minutes.

CHANTERELLE RISOTTO

MAKES 4 TO 6 SERVINGS

In our house, risotto is our go-to meal. When chanterelles are not in season, I use whatever mushrooms I can find at the store. I always have dried chanterelles, shiitakes or morels on hand, so I soak those up, saving the soaking liquid to cook with. We use an Instant Pot to make our daily risotto, following the steps in this recipe up to adding the broth. I add 4 cups of broth, close the lid and program the cooker for 5 minutes at high pressure. However, if you have time, there is nothing more romantic and relaxing than making risotto the old-fashioned way.

- 1 pound fresh chanterelles
- 2 tablespoons plus 2 tablespoons unsalted butter, divided
- salt, to taste
- fresh ground pepper, to taste
- 1 medium yellow onion, diced
- 2 cloves garlic, minced
- 2 cups Arborio rice
- ½ cup white wine
- 4–5 cups mushroom broth
- 1 cup grated Parmigiano-Reggiano and extra for garnish
- 2 tablespoons chopped parsley
- 1 lemon, sliced in half

Pick off any dirty pieces from the chanterelles and clean with a wet towel. Thickly slice the mushrooms. In a large nonstick sauté pan, melt 2 tablespoons butter over medium heat. Add mushrooms and sauté for 5 to 7 minutes until liquid evaporates and mushrooms are slightly browned. Season with salt and pepper to taste. Transfer mushrooms to a bowl and set aside.

Heat 2 tablespoons butter in the same pan over medium heat. Add onion and garlic, and salt and pepper to taste. Cook, stirring, until onions are translucent, about 5 minutes. Add the rice and cook, stirring for about 2 minutes. Add wine and cook until liquid absorbs. Stir in mushrooms and cook for 1 minute.

Add 1 cup broth and cook until liquid absorbs, about 2 to 3 minutes. Repeat, adding broth until 1 cup remains. Then add ½ cup, if necessary. Rice should be just tender and not raw, and risotto should have a rich sauce. Add remaining broth until desired doneness. Remove from heat and stir in the cheese and parsley. Scoop into individual bowls, squeeze some lemon juice on top, garnish with cheese and serve immediately.

ROAST PORK CHOPS WITH GRAPES, GOOSEBERRIES AND ROSEMARY

SERVES 4

We planted a gooseberry bush this year, which excites me to no end. I discovered these green beauties in my college days hiking in the Sierra Nevada Mountains. I became enamored of the seedy, slightly tart berries, and on my hikes I hoped to find some evidence of the treasures. Sometimes I wondered if my attraction to them was because of the care needed to harvest them, as they harbor wicked thorns. I still believe that all good things in life take some effort to find and keep. However, the Pixwell variety we have growing in our yard is nearly thornless, and it was a pleasure to harvest my few cups of berries this year. Imagine my surprise when I went to the summer's first Yellowstone Valley Farmers' Market in downtown Billings to find the Martinsdale Colony selling generous bags of gooseberries.

The secret to juicy pork is the brining. You can, of course, throw everything into a baking dish without the brining and searing. These extra steps enhance the texture, flavor and color of the dish, but it is still delicious if you choose to just assemble everything without the fuss. If you do this, just season with a little more salt and bake for a bit longer. If you want, substitute chicken breasts for the pork. Just remember, though, that thoroughly cooked chicken will register an internal temperature of 165°F.

FOR THE BRINE

2 cups water

¼ cup kosher salt

3 tablespoons brown sugar

2 cloves garlic, peeled and crushed

2 cups ice

3 tablespoons extra virgin olive oil, divided

4 bone-in pork chops, each about ¾ inch thick

2 cups seedless green grapes

1 cup green gooseberries

1 small white onion, halved and thinly sliced

4 cloves garlic, sliced

¼ cup fresh rosemary leaves

1 teaspoon salt

fresh ground black pepper, to taste

In a medium saucepan, bring 2 cups of water to a boil. Add salt, brown sugar and garlic. Stir until salt and sugar are dissolved. Remove pan from heat and add ice. If mixture is still hot, let it come to room temperature. Place pork in a large, self-sealing bag, add brine, seal bag and refrigerate for 6 to 24 hours. Remove chops from the brine, discarding brine, and pat chops dry with paper towels.

Heat olive oil in large skillet over medium-high heat, sear pork chops, about 2 minutes on each side. Set aside.

Drizzle 1 tablespoon olive oil onto the bottom of a 9x13-inch baking dish. Layer half the grapes, gooseberries, onion, garlic and rosemary onto the bottom of the dish. Place pork chops on top of onion mixture. Layer the rest of the onion, garlic and rosemary on top of the chops. Drizzle remaining olive oil across the top. Season with salt and pepper, to taste.

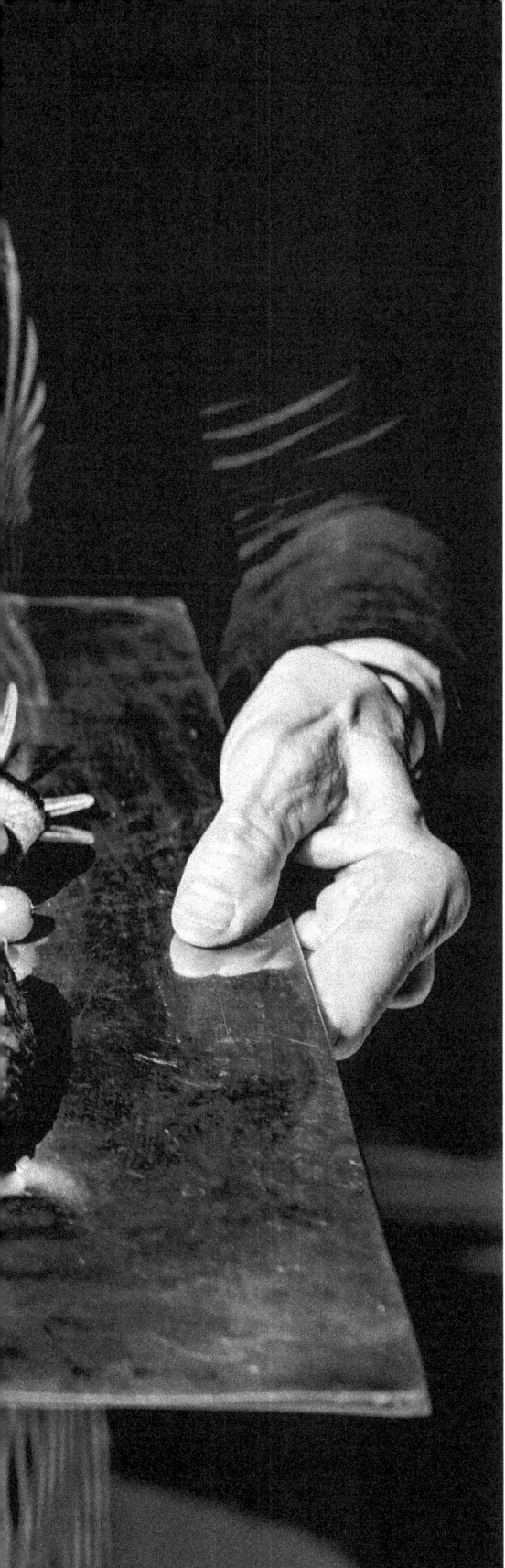

Heat oven to 375°F. Bake for 25 minutes and, using an instant-read thermometer, take the internal temperature of the pork. When the temperature reaches 140°F, take the dish out of the oven and cover with foil, letting pork rest while its temperature rises to 145°F for properly cooked pork. Serve immediately.

COOK'S NOTES

Not gooseberry season? Use green grapes for the entire dish and, for fun, throw in some seedless red grapes.

DOUBLE CHOCOLATE ROSE HIP MUFFINS

MAKES 1 DOZEN

Roses and chocolate are redolent of romance. This recipe was created to use up the pulp left over from making **Rose Hip Syrup** *for the* **Rose Hip Baklava**. *I did not want to waste this earthy and subtly floral ingredient. Chocolate was a natural pairing.*

- 2 cups all-purpose flour
- 1 cup sugar
- ⅓ cup unsweetened cocoa powder
- 1½ teaspoons baking powder
- ½ teaspoon baking soda
- ¼ teaspoon salt
- 1 cup buttermilk
- ⅓ cup oil
- 2 eggs
- 1 teaspoon vanilla extract
- ½ cup semisweet chocolate chips
- ⅔ cup rose hips, coarsely chopped (see Cook's Notes)

Heat oven to 400°F. Grease 12 muffin cups or line with baking cups. Set aside.

Stir together flour, sugar, cocoa powder, baking powder, baking soda and salt in a large bowl. In another bowl, whisk together buttermilk, oil, eggs and vanilla extract. Pour wet mixture into dry mixture. Stir until just combined. Fold in chocolate chips and rose hips. Scoop into prepared muffin cups, filling ¾ full.

Bake until toothpick inserted into the middle comes out clean, about 20 minutes. Cool for 5 minutes in pan on wire rack. Remove muffins from pan and cool completely on wire rack. Store tightly covered at room temperature.

COOK'S NOTES

Rehydrate ½ cup dried rose hips with 1 cup boiling water. Let sit for 15 minutes or use the pulp leftover from making rose hip syrup for **Rose Hip Baklava**.

ROSE HIP BAKLAVA

MAKES ABOUT 40 PIECES

When hiking in the mountains in early summer, pretty pink alpine roses pop against the green grass and the snow not yet melted on the higher peaks. But I love seeing the bright red rose hips that form after the flower petals drop off later in the summer. They have the essence of rose mixed with bramble and touches of sour. The smell reminds me of crab apples. This recipe takes some time to assemble, so have everything ready before you get started.

FOR THE SYRUP

- 1½ cups **Rose Hip Syrup**
- ½ cup honey
- 1 tablespoon rose water
- 1 tablespoon lime juice

FOR THE BAKLAVA

- 1.1 pounds (17.3 ounces) phyllo dough, thawed
- 2 cups shelled raw pistachios, finely chopped
- 3 tablespoons sugar
- 1 teaspoon ground cardamom
- ¼ teaspoon ground nutmeg
- ¼ teaspoon salt
- ½ pound (2 sticks) unsalted butter, melted

Preheat oven to 325°F. Brush a 9x13-inch baking dish with some of the melted butter, about 2 tablespoons. Set aside.

In a small saucepan, bring the syrup and honey to a boil. Reduce heat and simmer for 20 minutes. Remove from the heat and stir in rose water and lime juice. Set aside.

Lay out phyllo dough on a cutting board. If necessary, cut the sheets to fit the baking pan. Save the leftover dough in the freezer for another recipe. Cover the dough with a towel to keep it from drying out.

In a medium bowl, mix together pistachios, sugar, cardamom, nutmeg and salt. Set aside.

To assemble, place eight layers of phyllo sheets in the pan one by one, brushing lightly with butter between each sheet. Spread one-fifth of the nut mixture on top of phyllo dough. Add another five layers of phyllo one by one, brushing each sheet with butter, and then add another fifth of nuts. The layer sequence of phyllo sheets should be 8, 5, 5, 5, 5, 8, with nuts spread in between the layers. Be sure to brush butter on the top layer.

Cut baklava into 1½-inch-wide strips. Then cut diagonally, about 1½ inches apart, to form diamond shapes.

Bake for about 1 hour on the center rack of the oven until edges and top are golden brown.

Bring syrup back to a boil just before baklava completes baking. Pour the hot syrup over the baklava. Let the baklava cool completely at room temperature for 8 hours (uncovered to prevent sogginess).

ROSE HIP SYRUP

MAKES ABOUT 1½ CUPS

Rose hips can be ordered online through Mountain Rose Herbs, but unsweetened cranberries can be substituted. Try this syrup on top of plain yogurt or, better yet, vanilla ice cream.

1 cup dried rose hips
3 cups water
½ cup sugar

Rinse rose hips and drain. Put rose hips into a medium saucepan with water and sugar. Bring to a boil and reduce heat to a simmer. Cook for 10 minutes until sugar has dissolved. Strain and keep in refrigerator until ready for use.

HUCKLEBERRY LEMON PUDDING CAKE

MAKES 10 PUDDINGS

I love this cake for its lemony goodness. Fresh huckleberries are best, but blueberries and blackberries can also be substituted. I secured my first huckleberries of this season from my friend and mentor Greg Patent and his wife, Dorothy, when we visited them in Missoula. They generously provided this mysterious dark berry that, when bitten into, bursts refreshing concentrated blueberry-flavored juice. For these cakes, I like tipping the berries to one side so the yellow color of the lemon pudding shines when you turn the cake onto a plate. My husband thinks this cake is best with crème anglaise, again inspired from our time with Greg and Dorothy. Greg made a carafe of this decadent sauce to pour over fresh berries, but better yet is his Rhubarb-Strawberry Pie that is found in his James Beard Award Foundation award-winning cookbook, Baking in America.

1½ tablespoons butter, softened
1 cup fresh huckleberries
2 teaspoons sugar plus ½ cup plus ½ cup sugar, divided
¼ teaspoon plus ¾ teaspoon minced lemon zest, divided
½ cup all-purpose flour
½ teaspoon baking powder
1½ cups buttermilk
½ cup lemon juice, about 4 lemons
2 egg yolks
4 egg whites
pinch of salt

Heat oven to 350°F. Butter ten 6-ounce ramekins or baking cups. Place cups in a 2-inch-deep baking pan and set aside. Boil a kettle of water.

In a small bowl, stir together huckleberries with 2 teaspoons sugar and ¼ teaspoon lemon zest. Spoon evenly into prepared cups. Tip berries to one side of the cups. Set aside.

In a large bowl, blend well flour, baking powder and ½ cup sugar. Stir in buttermilk, lemon juice, egg yolks and remaining lemon zest. Set aside.

With an electric mixer, beat the egg whites with salt until the whites foam and start to stiffen. Add remaining ½ cup sugar and beat until stiff peaks form. Fold whites into the batter. Spoon batter evenly into the prepared cups. Add boiling water into the baking pan until the water reaches halfway up the sides of the cups. Bake for 55 minutes until puffy and golden. Serve cake warm, at room temperature or cold right out of the cups, or invert onto a plate and serve with a dollop of whipped cream. The cakes can keep in the refrigerator for up to 5 days when tightly sealed. To invert, microwave for about 20 seconds or soak cup in some hot water to loosen the cold cake.

BEEF: FROM GATE TO PLATE

Over the years, *Flavors Under the Big Sky: Celebrating the Bounty of the Region* featured beef on several shows from farm to table, gate to plate and pasture to plate. I started in the field in one of the first shows I produced with Jackie Yamanaka. We attended the inaugural Raising the Steaks: 2016 Environmental Stewardship Ranch Tour, journeying to the American Fork Ranch in Two Dot, Montana, in the shadow of the Crazy Mountains. More recently, I talked with Shane and Tanya Flowers of Ranch House Sausage Company and Ranch House Meat Company, learning how the nice packages of meat end up at the grocery store and into the skillets in our kitchens.

The Rex Bar and Grill, located on Montana Avenue, symbolized the iconic place to get a steak when eating out. For me, it became synonymous with eating steak—I could taste beef along with history. I had the honor to speak with Gene Burgad, co-owner of The Rex Bar and Grill, and Executive Chef David Maplethorpe. Even before my husband and I moved to Billings, we went to The Rex to get a steak when we visited friends who lived in town. After settling here, The Rex was the go-to place for us to bring guests to show them Montana's biggest bounty.

ENVIRONMENTAL STEWARDSHIP RANCH TOUR

At the Environmental Stewardship Ranch Tour, about forty people, mostly ranchers, learned about how the health of rangeland, streams and creeks, as well as the wildlife, interplay and influence successful cattle ranching. I talked to rancher Lon Reukauf, a longtime Montana Stockgrowers Association and National Cattleman's Association member, who lives north of Miles City on Cherry Creek Ranch, and to Annie Evjene, the co-ranch manager of the American Fork Ranch.

Raising steak begins early, according to Reukauf. "All this process actually starts before the young animal is conceived. It's called prenatal nutrition, so you need to make sure that the mom is in really good shape and has a very complete diet and has good enough physical condition to handle the elements. It is the winter before the calf is conceived."

Reukauf continued, "The calf is conceived in the summer, born the following April. The nutrition of that calf and the vaccination programs are really important at a very young age. A lot of the quality is formed when that calf is at a very young age, or even before it is born. The nutrition of mom and the calf determines the marbling that you desire, not the waste fat."

As with growing produce, the production of cattle followed the seasons. "We do not have nutritional challenges in the early summer when the calf is very young," Reukauf pointed out. "They move cattle to fresh pasture. Different pastures get used at different times during the year."

To accomplish the ultimate flavor, Reukauf said, "Grass finishing is more of the art, and it's important that the animal is harvested off of grass when the green period is beginning. It is a very narrow window this far north."

A cow's life cycle begins from birth, followed by weaning from its mother's milk. The calf continues to grow by grazing on grass and pastures. The calf can be auctioned off at this point, or earlier, after weaning. Mature cattle can move to feedlots or feed yards to be fed a balanced diet of roughage, grain and local renewable resources, such as potato peels or sugar beet tops. Once a cow reaches market weight of about 1,200 to 1,400 pounds, it goes to the packing plant.

At Montana Ale Works in Bozeman, Executive Chef Aaron Brittingham talked of acquiring locally sourced products: "We're a very large restaurant, and there is not quite enough in Bozeman to supply us with everything we need. We try to work with local farms and ranchers to get higher-quality produce and meats. Put our money back into the local economy."

Brittingham shared an example of how he has collaborated with Montana Wagyu Cattle Company to serve wagyu hamburgers. Because the company has no problem selling the higher-end cuts such as tenderloin, strip loins and ribeye, the restaurant now takes the ground meat.

In cooking the beef, Executive Chef Eric Trager of Old Piney Dell at Rock Creek Resort (currently at Carbon Fork in Red Lodge) confessed, "I really crave the flat iron. It's a different cut. It's affordable for most people. It's really tender and really good flavor."

In preparing the meat for cooking, Trager provided some examples. For the seasoning, "Salt and pepper, sometimes a little bit of fresh thyme. If it is a well-marbled cut of meat, I will grill it. If it tends to be a little leaner, I tend to pan sear it in a little clarified butter. Hotter temperature and sear in the juices. Brings out the strong flavors of the beef itself."

For the various cuts of meat, Trager had these instructions. For short ribs, he recommended searing the outside to caramelize, followed with slow braising in oven for four or five hours. Smoked brisket is first smoked in mesquite for six hours and then finished by braising in the oven for another six hours. For tenderloin, Trager pan sears the meat, seasoning with just salt and pepper and adding clarified butter to bring out more beef flavor. A rib eye or New York strip is usually grilled.

As far as thickness, Trager said, "The thicker the cut I can get a better temperature on the beef and can taste the full flavor of the beef than a real thin cut."

At the Homestead Bed and Breakfast in Big Timber, I sat down with Executive Chef Mike Erickson, culinary arts instructor at Burnet High School Culinary Arts Program. Erickson coproduced the movie *True Beef: From Pasture to Plate*. The film highlights Texas beef through the eyes of high school culinary and agricultural students.

Erickson started cooking while watching and helping his mom in the kitchen. At the time I spoke to him, students were watching *him* cook. Even though Erickson has received degrees from the Culinary Institute of America and Johnson and Wales University and has had a long culinary career, he admitted to constantly learning about new food. But to really learn to cook, Erickson advocated hands-on experience. He especially valued the old art of butchery.

In Helena, Chef Alan Michaud laid the groundwork to start the Montana Meat Collective, where consumers have an opportunity to source an animal from a local producer and then learn to butcher the animal into usable cuts and parts. Erickson advocated, "I think the number one thing is respect the food and respect the farmers and the ranchers." He concluded, "I thank God every day for the job I get to do. But I would not get to do what I like to do the last thirty years, whether it be teaching or cooking, without the farmers and ranchers of America."

RANCH HOUSE SAUSAGE COMPANY

Ranch House Sausage Company is located on the outskirts of Billings, right off Highway 312, just outside Shepherd, Montana. As it's a nondescript building, one could easily drive by it. But in this facility, with a 1,200-square-foot retail space, meat, seasonings, jerky and sausage are sold. Behind the store, thousands of pounds of meat are processed for consumption.

Shane and Tanya Flowers purchased the forty-year-old Project Meats, advertised as a "Retail Meat Sales and Slaughter House," in 2007. When Shane and his wife bought the business, it was solely a custom processing plant. In wanting a more understandable and universal name, they renamed the business to Ranch House Sausage Company, and in 2014, they opened a small market in midtown Billings called Ranch House Meat Company but now have moved to the West End. To be true to their name, they started making sausages and bacon, along with beef sticks and jerky, as well as custom butchering of hogs, cattle and wild game.

Growing up in Cody, Wyoming, Shane was surrounded with the ranching lifestyle, with family members working in the agricultural business. When recollecting college at Northwest College in Powell, he said, "I took some meat cutting courses down there, but my big passion was business, not necessarily the meat side, but I was always looking for a business to get into." He admitted to knowing little about the meat processing business, but he and Tanya quickly learned firsthand every aspect of their company.

"I committed myself, and Tanya as well, and it didn't matter if it meant cleaning the floors or washing knives, we did everything here. When we first started, we had about eight employees here, and we decided we needed to streamline a few processes," trimming the staff to six. At that time, when business was slow in March or April, the Flowerses gave employees paid time off, but times have changed.

"We always have something to do," Shane said. Whether custom processing, butchering after fairs or getting product ready for the holiday seasons, they are always busy. With business taking on a rapid growth, Ranch House Sausage Company now only accepts wild game that has been cleaned, whereas in years past, they took in whole animals brought in by hunters. During a year, Shane estimated that "on the average, a beef is about 1,400 pounds live, 800 pounds hanging weight, so you're talking about 800,000, 900,000 pounds of beef" that is processed per year.

The main spaces in the plant include the harvest room and the production room. Next to the production room is a large cold room where carcass halves hang before they are cut into smaller portions. In the production room, two grinders, a saw and packaging equipment are housed.

Bacon is one of the popular products the company sells. The company offers fourteen different flavors, ranging from garlic pepper and honey maple to jalapeño and cinnamon apple. Shane said, "We have something for everybody, but everyone looks for lean, and fat is actually what carries the flavor of bacon." To establish the selection, Tanya said, "We have a little support group that likes to come and give us their ideas."

The Flowerses have brought in equipment to help accelerate and facilitate the processing of their meats. A vacuum tumbler is used to accelerate the curing of bacon and hams processed at the facility. Shane said, "We can cure bacon in about two hours and hams in four hours, whereas it used to be weeks to cure that kind of stuff."

After curing, the meats can be smoked or injected with flavor. The Flowerses have a machine, about the size of a large oven, with a conveyor belt and a dozen hypodermic needles. Meats are injected with flavoring rather than sitting in a marinade for days.

With three smokehouses, Shane shared, "We can do thousands of pounds of product in a day. We've got some product that is smoked-cooked in four hours. There are products that take twelve to fourteen hours to take through the whole process." Two of the smokers look like large steel refrigerators. The largest one is reminiscent of a small closet that could hold six adults standing side by side. The machinery is programmable for consistency and customization.

Wood chips, about the size of sawdust, dominated, with hickory wood burned in a hopper and the smoke flowing through a hose into the smoking chamber.

The piece of equipment that Shane may be most proud of is the bacon slicer. The machine takes thirty seconds to slice a side of bacon, making it faster than any human could accomplish the job.

Ranch House Sausage Company dedicates a single room to sausage making. "We built this room several years ago and brought in some pretty top-end equipment from manufacturers to process as quickly and effectively as we can," Shane said. "Everything is measured down to the hundredth of a pound, as far as seasonings and all those kind of things. With this type of technology, the consumer also knows exactly what goes into their product."

On this day, two men inserted ground meat into casings. Once the sausages are put on trays, they go into the smoker. Cellulose and collagen casings are used to provide more uniform results. "These guys can make about two hundred pounds in forty-five minutes, filling the smokehouse, rotating the smokehouses a couple times during the day."

Ranch House Sausage Company also makes jerky and snack sticks. "We do more snack sticks than any other product, hands down. Snack sticks are about 75 percent of the smoked product that come from this facility."

In 2014, the Flowerses opened a retail space in Billings in the shopping center adjacent to what was then the IGA grocery store. The couple worked with a realtor and did a market study, concluding that the midtown location, situated near two grocery stores, was a strategic spot.

"We wanted to bring the country into town, so we have a lot of wood things in here, a lot of bucket lights." The space is reminiscent of a ranch house, filled with coziness and playful displays and products organized by type, such as pork and beef. The highlight of the store may be in the back, where the boldly labeled "Baconapolis" reigns, with three coolers dedicated to fourteen flavors of thick-cut bacon. The fresh cuts are located in a cooler named "Carnivore's Cuts."

Next to the meats, Tanya has placed items such as seasoning, sauces and pasta that can be served with the meat. "We have things that complement the meats. We have marinara sauce near our hot Italian sausage, if you are making spaghetti."

Five years later, they closed the midtown location and moved west to the Shiloh Crossing area.

THE REX BAR AND GRILL

The Rex Bar and Grill closed the day after Valentine's Day 2018, after the Rex partnership decided to shut down the restaurant with no advance notice to the community. A handwritten sign on the door announced its closing.

During The Rex's thirty-four years of operation, Gene Burgad was the face of the restaurant, backed by two silent partners. Executive Chef David Maplethorpe ran the kitchen for twenty-seven of those years. He had hoped to retire in May 2018 but was forced to move that date forward with the sudden closing. The partners decided that the time was right to quit the restaurant and bar, while continuing to lease offices in the upper floors of the former hotel.

H. Alfred Heimer opened the Rex Hotel and Bar across from the Billings Depot on March 27, 1909, with the help of his friend "Buffalo Bill" Cody. At sixteen, the German immigrant took a job with Buffalo Cody's Wild West Show in 1894. The young man, who was purportedly fired three times, worked for Cody in his private railway car until 1903.

In 1975, Senia Hart saved The Rex from demolition by purchasing the dilapidated historic building. Later, she sold it to A&E Architects, which later sold to Gene Burgad and his partners. To this day, the mahogany bar with brass foot railings, the metal ceiling and the stained and beveled glass windows remain.

In 1917, a third-floor addition converted Heimer's hotel into one of the best places to stay at the time. Noteworthy guests included the Crow Chief Plenty Coups, heading to Washington, D.C., in 1921. More colorful celebrities included Will James and Calamity Jane.

During Prohibition, festivities moved from room to room at the hotel. Underground tunnels provided for the movement of alcohol and parties. Gambling and prostitution were popular pastimes during the period.

If only the walls could talk. Reid Pyburn—who started at The Rex as a dishwasher and worked his way up by bartending and managing the restaurant—recalled ghost stories. During October, in the weeks before Halloween, tours would come through in search of a ghost named "Buck" and a woman that occupied the lower floors who was reportedly seen by guests as they descended the stairway.

Pyburn's firsthand experience came when a couple came in for dinner one night. They were coincidentally seated at table 13, and Pyburn was asked by a waiter to come to the table. The female guest requested a table change because she saw a ghost standing by the table. After the staff moved the diners, the woman said, "This sort of thing happens to me all the time."

Tolerance of ghosts is a testimonial to the loyalty of local patrons. Throughout the years, celebrities and dignitaries, as well as locals, gathered at The Rex. Clint Eastwood showed up for the opening of the patio when Burgad and his partners closed down Twenty-Fourth Street North to expand the restaurant. The massive oval bar, large beamed ceilings and outside patio with a fire pit were added during this remodel.

The soft opening turned into a major event with Eastwood's presence. Hostess Krissy Duenow recalled that throughout the years she waited on customers such as Mel Gibson

and Sawyer Brown. Vice President Dan Quayle also ate at the restaurant. When *Far and Away* was being filmed in the Depot across the street, production crew dined frequently at the restaurant. Burgad and Maplethorpe remembered seeing Tom Cruise and Nicole Kidman in the establishment.

Although there was always excitement in seeing famous patrons, Maplethorpe, Pyburn and Duenow all emphasized that the staff treated everyone fairly. Pyburn said, "That is why celebrities liked coming there because no one bothered them." Maplethorpe added, "They were just customers; they all had to be treated the same."

With years of working together, the staff felt like family. In pursuing the goal of satisfying customers, front of house and back of house worked together. Service required physical and mental agility, with everyone working as a team. The joint effort brought camaraderie, bonding them through good times and also challenging ones. Together, they pushed through the long hours and late nights.

Over the years, The Rex contributed to the community by hosting the Guest Chefs Dinners for the Montana State University Billings Foundation Wine and Food Festival. Chefs such as Bernard Guillas, Kevin Davis, Emily Luchetti and Shane Ryan have cooked in the kitchen alongside Maplethorpe to raise funds for scholarships.

Black angus beef highlighted the menu. Steaks were seasoned with salt and pepper, accompanied with a cognac Dijon mustard sauce, mushroom sauce, garlic butter, peppered or plain. Prime rib rubbed with spices came to the table served plain or blackened. According to Maplethorpe, the most popular item on the menu was the Garlic Roasted Fillet, topped with the cognac Dijon mustard sauce. He jokingly shared that he disliked the dish but could not take it off the menu for fear of a customer revolt. Duenow remembered the popular warm loaves of fresh-baked bread, brought to the table on a cutting board.

Years of serving beef brought recognition to the restaurant by the National Cattlemen's Beef Association through the 2007 National Foodservice Beef Backer Award. Maplethorpe said he was proud to receive "Innovator of the Year" in recognition of his skills.

Burgad was almost always present, watching over the business and greeting customers. Employees respected how he handled the intense day-to-day demands of the business. Duenow recalled one incident where a conflict was resolved by a simple "walk around the block" with Burgad. "I always knew if I needed anything in the world, he would be there for me." Duenow left the business almost twenty-five years ago but still had this to say: "I miss Gene a lot. He was very good to me.

Pyburn recalled, "One thing I learned from Gene was not to overreact, not to get mad. Empower your employees to make decisions." Now, as the owner of the High Horse Saloon and Eatery, he believes that an owner needs to set an example and perform all duties that he expects his employees to do.

Maplethorpe spent the majority of his daily hours at the restaurant, and Burgad became a very good friend. Those who worked there became his family. Retired from the rigors of being a chef, Maplethorpe remains in the business as chef/culinary jobs skills instructor for the Billings Food Bank.

Rick Larson and his family recently bought The Rex. The restaurant has been renamed Buffalo Block at The Rex. Buffalo Block refers to the durable bricks found in the building. The name also gives "Buffalo Bill" Cody a nod for investing in the beginnings of The Rex.

The Larson family wanted to preserve the historic restaurant that held fond memories for them. Larson had been going regularly to The Rex since 1980 in search of a good steak. He traveled to Denver and Chicago to study steakhouses, wanting to open a restaurant serving high-end steaks. Some ideas included a showcase refrigerator in the restaurant for aging meat and a wood-fired grill for cooking up steaks.

As a new chapter begins for The Rex, Burgad expressed gratitude for his co-workers: "Great people, working both with and for the customers. I can't say enough about the customers." "We will both miss it, but we must go on," Maplethorpe concluded.

The world lost Gene Burgad on August 14, 2019. The Billings community will miss the man who greeted those who came to eat and drink at The Rex. I know I will miss his self-deprecating sense of humor, generosity and hugs. He brought flavor and deliciousness to Billings that will not be soon forgotten.

PART IV
PLAINS

The Great Plains in Montana is the immense expanse of grasslands stretching from the Rocky Mountains to the Missouri River. The region once known as the "Great American Desert" has been referred to as the "Heartland" or the "Breadbasket of the World." The plains extend over vast distances with sparse population, allowing for unobstructed views and, in my head, room to think.

Few trees grow in the vast semi-desert plains except near rivers and lakes. Silver sagebrush and wheatgrass cover this landscape. I've always believed that winds are high here because there is nothing to stop the movement. Weather in the Great Plains varies from very cold and harsh winters to very hot summers.

Agriculture, including both crops and livestock, is Montana's largest industry and happens in the plains. Cattle ranching has been central to Montana's history and economy since the 1800s. Wheat is the state's leading crop. Hay and barley are important crops, as are lentils, peas, chickpeas, canola, corn, safflower, oats and sugar beets.

In this section, the largest in the book, I share the recipes that most reflect my time living in Billings. I want to pay homage to what I overlooked when I first moved here, but I have become enamored of the bounty here, as well as of the food and talent. The recipes were influenced from what I discovered at the Yellowstone Farmers' Market and local grocery stores, as well as what my husband grows in our garden. This is why I have included, in the second half of this section, multiple ways to cook some of my favorite vegetables that we bring into the kitchen over the summer.

CHIVE DUTCH BABY

MAKES 4 TO 8 SERVINGS

A Dutch baby baking in the oven is worth watching through the window, for it is the ultimate show of eggs cooking. The batter puffs up on the rim of the skillet in a round ridge, transforming to a golden brown color as it bakes. When it emerges from the oven, it is most impressive but does quickly collapse, as though taking a bow after a performance. Use your imagination for the toppings, from fresh herbs to capers, smoked salmon, cooked sausage or crème fraîche.

3 tablespoons unsalted butter, cut into 6 pieces
½ cup whole milk
¼ cup heavy cream
3 large eggs
½ teaspoon salt
fresh ground black pepper, a good grind
¾ cup all-purpose flour
¼ cup coarsely cut chives

FOR THE TOPPING
ricotta cheese
grated Manchego cheese (or a cheese of your choosing)
fresh micro greens such as kale, sunflower or beet microgreens

Heat oven to 425°F. Place butter in a 10-inch ovenproof seasoned cast-iron or heavy nonstick skillet.

In a blender, add milk, cream, eggs, salt and pepper. Puree until blended. Add the flour and blend, scraping sides and bottom for an even mixing. Add chives and pulse a few times to incorporate.

Put skillet into the middle rack of the oven and bake until butter melts and bubbles. Pour batter into the hot skillet and slide back into the oven.

Bake for 20 to 25 minutes until pancake is golden brown and puffs up around the edge of the skillet. The middle of the pancake will be slightly puffed. Quickly dollop some ricotta into the center along with sprinkles of cheese and microgreens. Slide onto a large warm platter or cut into slices and serve immediately.

BIG SKY BISON BURGER WITH BLUE CHEESE, CARAMELIZED ONIONS AND BACON

SERVES 4

A bison burger with blue cheese, caramelized onions and bacon is my idea of a Big Sky burger. This sustaining combination exudes robust flavors. Bison burgers are best served medium rare, as the lean meat is easy to overcook. This is in keeping with the Yellowstone Public Radio motto of "A rare medium, well done."

*The key is to sandwich everything inside a soft brioche or pretzel bun to ensure you have a fighting chance at containing all the goodness. The salty blue cheese, crisp, peppery bacon and sweet and sour caramelized onions from the **Caramelized Onion Jam** make for wonderful accompaniments to the meaty yet lean patty.*

4 slices peppered bacon, cut in half

1¼ pounds ground bison

salt, to taste

fresh ground black pepper, to taste

2 tablespoons butter plus 2 tablespoons unsalted butter, divided, softened

4 brioche or pretzel buns

2 tablespoons mayonnaise

4 green leaf lettuce leaves

4 slices tomato

½ cup crumbled blue cheese

4 tablespoons **Caramelized Onion Jam**

In a skillet, lay out bacon pieces without touching or overlapping. Cook over medium heat. Turn the pieces as needed until they reach desired crispness, 8 to 12 minutes. Set bacon aside on paper towels.

Form ground bison into 4 patties larger than the bun, as the meat shrinks as it cooks. Season with salt and black pepper, to taste. Top each burger with ½ tablespoon butter.

Heat skillet to medium-high heat or grill to medium high. Cook patty until bottom browns, about 5 minutes. Then flip. Top with blue cheese and bacon and cook until desired doneness, with medium rare measuring an internal temperature of 135°F, or about 5 minutes. While patty is cooking, spread butter on the insides of the buns. Lightly brown on buttered side down in skillet or on the grill.

To assemble, spread mayonnaise on the bottom of the bun and top with lettuce, tomato, patty, blue cheese, bacon, onions and the top of the bun.

BISON SIRLOIN STEAKS WITH COFFEE COCOA RUB

MAKES 2 TO 4 SERVINGS

*Steaks are synonymous with summer, with bison steaks epitomizing the season in our land under the Big Sky. However, firing up the grill in the winter can be satisfying, if not convenient or efficient. When my husband grills in the winter, he believes he is defying Mother Nature and conquering the dropping temperatures. This rub has really earthy flavors, and when it's pressed onto bison or beef and grilled, savory caramel characteristics emerge. The bison steak is best served medium rare, as it is leaner than beef and can be tough if overcooked. The steak, sliced thinly, is excellent for sandwiches the next day with **Caramelized Onions** or **Rhubarb Chutney**.*

- 4 1-pound sirloin bison steaks, about half an inch thick
- ⅓ cup **Coffee Cocoa Seasoning Rub**
- 2 tablespoons extra virgin olive oil or melted butter

> **COOK'S NOTES**
>
> For additional flavor dimensions, add 1 tablespoon powdered mustard along with 1 teaspoon of cloves and ½ teaspoon of cinnamon, or more chili powder if you want more kick.

About 20 minutes before grilling, remove the steaks from the refrigerator and allow them to sit, covered, at room temperature. In a bowl, add seasoning rub and set aside.

Heat the grill to high. Brush steaks on both sides with oil and sprinkle rub generously on both sides. Place the steaks on the grill and cook until golden brown and slightly charred, 4 to 5 minutes. Turn the steaks over and continue to grill about 3 to 4 minutes for medium rare (or an internal temperature of 135°F), 5 to 7 minutes for medium (140°F) or 8 to 10 minutes for medium well (150°F).

Transfer the steaks to a platter or cutting board, tent loosely with foil and let rest for 5 minutes before slicing. Slice and serve.

LINZER COOKIES WITH CHOKECHERRY JAM

MAKES 12 COOKIES

The first cookies I learned to make from scratch were the traditional Linzer cookies from Germany. The recipe came from a cookbook I borrowed from the library. This particular cookie recipe developed from my love of bringing together dessert wine, cheese and cookies. When we moved to Montana, I learned to embrace goat cheese, becoming acquainted with a cheese that was creamy yet crumbly, with tang and an earthy funkiness. The cheese pairs beautifully with a Sauvignon Blanc, which is usually my wine of choice. The brisk and refreshing wine with notes of grapefruit and grass is a good match with goat cheese.

To end a meal, I always enjoy serving dessert and a sweet wine. These cookies, with the combination of buttery goodness and nutty, savory and herb notes, make for a yummy combination with a glass of port.

¼ cup fresh goat cheese
1 egg yolk
zest from 1 lemon
1 teaspoon vanilla
1¼ cups all-purpose flour
¾ cup almond flour
½ cup sugar
¼ teaspoon salt
⅔ cup unsalted butter
2 teaspoons fresh rosemary leaves
confectioners' sugar, for dusting
chokecherry jam

Line baking sheet with parchment paper. Set aside.

In a small bowl, mix together goat cheese, egg yolk, lemon zest and vanilla. Set aside.

Into a food processor bowl, add flour, almond flour, sugar, salt and more lemon zest. Pulse to combine. Add the butter and pulse until dough forms pieces that look like large peas. Add goat cheese mixture and rosemary. Pulse until the dough comes together.

Roll dough out on lightly floured surface to about ¼-inch thickness. Cut out the cookies with a 2½-inch round cookie cutter, about 12 cookies. Gather dough and cut 12 more cookies, this time using a small cookie cutter to cut an opening in the center. Place sheet of cookies in the refrigerator for 30 minutes to chill.

Heat oven to 350°F. Bake cookies for 8 to 10 minutes or until edges are just beginning to brown. Cool on baking sheet for 5 minutes. Transfer cookies to a rack to cool completely.

Dust tops of cookies that have cut outs with confectioners' sugar. Spoon jam on the whole cookies and then top with the sugar-dusted cookies.

BEETS, OLIVES, MINT AND DUKKAH SALAD WITH ORANGE VINAIGRETTE
SERVES 4 TO 6

This salad is lovely in appearance and pretty in flavor. Most of us do not think of eating beets raw, but they have a wonderful crunch and sweetness. Aside from the red variety, try yellow and red-white striped.

FOR THE VINAIGRETTE
- ¼ cup orange juice
- 2 tablespoons balsamic vinegar
- 1 teaspoon Dijon mustard
- 2 teaspoons honey

- 1 pound small beets, about 4 to 5, cleaned, peeled, julienned
- 1 orange, skin removed, quartered, sliced
- ½ cup seedless Kalamata olives, halved lengthwise
- ¼ cup torn mint leaves
- 3 tablespoons **Dukkah**
- fresh ground black pepper, to taste

In a small bowl, whisk together vinaigrette ingredients. Set aside. In a medium bowl, toss beets, orange, olive, mint and Dukkah with vinaigrette. Season with black pepper to taste. Serve immediately.

ROASTED BEET PESTO

MAKES ABOUT 1 CUP

Roasted beet pesto is delicious spread on a toasted bagel or tossed with penne pasta.

4 to 5 **Roasted Beets**
½ cup roasted walnuts
3 stalks green onions
½ cup feta cheese
1 tablespoon lemon juice
¼ cup extra virgin olive oil
salt, to taste
fresh ground pepper, to taste

Into a food processor bowl, add beets, walnuts and green onions. Pulse several times until beets and nuts are minced. Add cheese and lemon juice. Pulse several times, making sure to scrape the sides. While processor is running, add oil in a steady stream. Process until all ingredients are incorporated. Season with salt and black pepper, to taste.

ROASTED BEETS

SERVES 2 TO 4

1 pound small beets, about 4 to 5, cleaned, skins on

Heat oven to 425°F. Put beets in a baking dish and cover. Bake until beets are slightly soft to the touch, 45 minutes to 1 hour, depending on their size. Cool beets and then rub off skins with your fingers and peel with a knife, if necessary. Store in refrigerator for up to a week in an airtight container.

WHOLE ROASTED CARROTS

SERVES 4 TO 8

Roasting carrots brings out a sweet caramel flavor in them. When carrots are roasted without peeling, they cook with their flavor sealed in their own skins. They make a delicious addition to a green salad, or they can be chopped up and mixed into a pot of farro or brown rice. Add a teaspoon of toasted cumin or dashes of cayenne during baking and finish with chopped mint, dill or oregano for added deliciousness.

Roasting carrots whole was inspired by Chef Nick Steen at Walkers Grill in downtown Billings. He served carrots with his pork featuring chicharrones, pork cheeks and pork shoulder in chile verde. Steen revamped the restaurant's menu for its twentieth anniversary in the spring of 2018. He cooks with flavors from around the world, while honoring the bounty of the region.

8 medium carrots, tops trimmed
2 teaspoons extra virgin olive oil
4 cloves garlic, minced
salt, to taste
fresh ground black pepper, to taste

Heat oven to 375°F. In a large bowl, toss unpeeled carrots with olive oil, garlic, salt and black pepper. Spread on baking sheet and bake for 1 hour or until center is tender when tested with a knife.

ROASTED CARROTS WITH TURMERIC AND CORIANDER

SERVES 4 AS A SIDE DISH

At your next gathering, place pieces of roasted carrot on a Chinese soup spoon. Garnish them with herbs with a dollop of sour cream, and I promise your guests will look at carrots differently.

3 cups coarsely chopped **Whole Roasted Carrots**
3 tablespoons chopped cilantro
2 tablespoons orange juice
¼ teaspoon ground turmeric
¼ teaspoon ground coriander
fresh ground black pepper, to taste
salt, to taste

In a medium bowl, toss together carrots, cilantro, orange juice, turmeric and coriander. Season with black pepper and salt to taste.

COLD CARROT GINGER SOUP

SERVES 4 AS A MAIN SOUP OR 6 TO 8 AS AN ACCOMPANIMENT

Enjoy this soup cold or hot. If heating up, bring it just to a boil and serve. Garnishing the soup with a dollop of sour cream or with chopped green onions or cilantro makes for a nice finish. Serve this with a toasted slice of bread brushed with olive oil or slathered with butter and rubbed with garlic.

3 cups coarsely chopped **Whole Roasted Carrots**
4 cups vegetable stock (add more or less stock depending on desired thickness)
½-inch thumb-sized ginger, peeled, coarsely sliced
1 teaspoon lime juice
⅛ teaspoon ground cardamom
salt, to taste

Put carrots, 3 cups of stock, ginger, lime juice and cardamom in a blender. Blend until smooth, adding more stock if you want to puree the soup to your desired thickness. Put blender container into the refrigerator to chill the soup, about 30 minutes. Then divide into bowls, garnishing with fresh herbs and a small sprinkle of salt on top.

ASIAN CARROT SLAW

SERVES 4

The addition of 1 teaspoon of minced ginger or jalapeño or 1 tablespoon of chopped cilantro or mint will give this salad another fresh dimension. Add shredded cabbage, jicama or radish for added crunch.

- ¾ pound carrots
- 3 stalks green onions, thinly sliced
- 2 tablespoons rice vinegar
- 1 tablespoon toasted sesame oil or vegetable oil
- ½ teaspoon lime juice
- ⅛ teaspoon salt or to taste
- 1 tablespoon toasted sesame seeds

Peel and trim carrots. Cut carrots into thin matchsticks or use a mandolin or shredder. Put cut carrots into a medium bowl. Add green onions, rice vinegar, sesame oil, lime juice and salt. Sprinkle in sesame seeds, toss and serve.

BABA GHANOUSH (ROASTED EGGPLANT DIP)

MAKES ABOUT 2 CUPS

This is one of those dips that, when set out among other dips without fanfare and attention, gets discovered and loved by those who are eggplant-averse. The traditional baba ghanoush is made with tahini or sesame paste, so even a few tablespoons of tahini would be delicious. Serve baba ghanoush with **Dukkah**, *a spice and nut combination that will be a perfect accompaniment.*

Japanese and Chinese eggplants are slender and long with thinner skin compared to the Western or Italian versions, which are more globe-shaped, with the latter smaller in size. When cooked up, the flesh of the Asian eggplants are almost creamy, while the other is thicker in texture and more fibrous.

20 ounces Japanese or Chinese eggplants, about 4 to 6, halved lengthwise
1 large shallot, with skin, halved
4 cloves garlic, with peel
3 tablespoons extra virgin olive oil
1 teaspoon salt
fresh ground black pepper
2 tablespoons lemon juice
⅓ cup chopped cilantro
salt, to taste

Heat oven to 400°F. Line a baking sheet with parchment paper. Place eggplant peel side down on prepared baking sheet. Place shallot on sheet with cut side down, along with garlic cloves. Brush vegetables with olive oil. Sprinkle with salt and a generous grind of black pepper. Bake for 30 minutes or until eggplant is soft. If the eggplant is light in color, broil for 2 minutes to give it a light golden color. Let cool to room temperature.

Remove flesh of eggplant from the skin. Discard the skin and put flesh into the food processor bowl. Discard skin of shallot and place in processor bowl. Squeeze out garlic cloves into bowl and discard skin. Pulse several times until everything is blended and still slightly chunky. Scoop mixture into a medium bowl. Stir in lemon juice and cilantro. Season with salt, to taste.

COOK'S NOTES

No Japanese or Chinese eggplants? Use Western or Italian eggplants instead. Slice the eggplant in half and poke flesh with a fork before drizzling with olive oil. Then you might need to bake the eggplant for 40 minutes before it softens.

ROASTED EGGPLANT

SERVES 4

about ¼ cup sesame oil

12 ounces Japanese or Chinese eggplants, about 3, cut lengthwise into ¼-inch slices

Heat broiler to high. Brush baking sheet with the sesame oil and place slices of eggplants on sheet. Then brush tops of eggplants with oil. Broil for about 3 minutes on highest rack until lightly browned and then turn eggplants over and broil other side for about 2 minutes or until lightly browned. Serve warm, room temperature or cold with **Thai Peanut Dipping Sauce.**

COOK'S NOTES

No Japanese or Chinese eggplants? Use a Western or Italian eggplants instead. You may need additional sesame oil, and you may need to cook the eggplant in several batches depending on size.

GRILLED ZUCCHINI

SERVES 4 AS A SIDE DISH

I believe zucchini is the king of the summer harvest. This is the vegetable that will grace office breakrooms, where gentlewoman farmers bring their surplus bounty. I have yet to set a chair out by an emerging zucchini, but I am confident that I would see it get bigger before my eyes. This is why so many giant zucchinis are harvested.

This is my favorite way to enjoy zucchini, especially if the grill is on for cooking other foods. Although plain extra virgin olive oil is my choice of oil for tossing before grilling, other oils can be used. There are a number of oils flavored with lemon or basil, for instance, that can be substituted in this recipe. Although I used only minced garlic here, think about using chopped herbs such as chives or dill that may be growing in your summer garden.

2 pounds zucchini, sliced lengthwise to ¼-inch thickness
2 tablespoons extra virgin olive oil
2 cloves garlic, minced
salt, to taste

Heat grill to high. Toss zucchini with oil, garlic and salt. Grill for about 3 minutes on each side to create grill marks and to desired doneness. Serve immediately or chilled.

ZUCCHINI PUREE

SERVES 4 TO 6

Pureed zucchini is a wonderful side to a grilled steak, roasted lamb or with steamed potatoes. This recipe can then be made into soup very easily by adding 4 cups of vegetable or chicken broth. The soup can be served chilled or heated with a slice of garlic bread or, better yet, toasted bread spread with pesto.

1 tablespoon extra virgin olive oil
1 small yellow onion, coarsely chopped
2 tablespoons fresh oregano leaves
salt, to taste
Grilled Zucchini

Heat oil over medium-high heat, add onion and sauté for about 2 minutes. Add oregano and salt and cook for another 3 minutes or until translucent. Set aside. Add grilled zucchini and cooked onions to a food processor. Process until smooth.

ZUCCHINI NOODLES

SERVES 4

A spiralizer is one of the "funky" tools I do have in my drawer, as it creates these long, beautiful zucchini noodles. If space is limited, the one slicing tool that is a must-have in my book is the mandoline, as it is versatile in cutting vegetables in countless ways.

1 pound zucchini, cut into noodles or shreds
1½ teaspoons capers, chopped
1 tablespoon lemon zest
1 tablespoon lemon juice
1 tablespoon extra virgin olive oil
¼ cup chopped chives
2 tablespoons mint, coarsely chopped
salt, to taste

In a large bowl, toss noodles with capers, lemon zest, lemon juice and olive oil. Then toss in chives and mint with a sprinkle of salt. Serve at room temperature or chilled.

EASY ZUCCHINI SAUTÉ

I would be remiss if I left this recipe out of this book, as it is my husband's most favorite way to cook zucchini. This dish can be finished off with chopped chives or chiffonade basil.

2 teaspoons extra virgin olive oil
2 cloves garlic, minced
1 or 2 zucchinis, about 1 pound, grated
salt, to taste
fresh ground black pepper, to taste
¼ cup grated Parmigiano-Reggiano

In a large skillet, heat oil over medium heat. Add garlic and cook until fragrant, about 1 minute. Add zucchini and sauté until just wilted, about 2 minutes. Season to taste with salt and pepper. Remove from heat and gently stir in cheese. Serve immediately.

ZUCCHINI FLOWER CORN SOUP

SERVES 4 TO 6

Corn reflects the sun and warmth of summer. There is nothing sweeter than an ear of corn eaten right after harvest, for it contains natural honest to goodness sugar created by Mother Nature. Better yet is grilled corn slathered with butter—for me, it may be mayonnaise instead.

Zucchini blossoms are another mirror of summer. The yellow-orange color of the flowers signals the emergence of the fruit. For gardeners, zucchini may be the most satisfying vegetable to grow. They grow big and fast. I am intrigued by the blossoms that are usually neglected, especially the boy variety, with the girl version turning into a squash. The blossoms add a creaminess to the soup along with light zucchini flavors and, of course, prettiness at the end as a garnish. Try the blossoms in a quesadilla with some mozzarella cheese drizzled with some **Roasted Tomatillo Salsa**.

4 ears fresh corn, silk and husks removed
2 tablespoons extra virgin olive oil
½ small white onion, sliced
2 cloves garlic, halved lengthwise
8 cups water
about 1 dozen zucchini flowers, stamens removed
1 medium Yukon potato, about 5 ounces, peeled, cut into 1-inch chunks
1 sprig thyme, leaves removed, stem discarded
1 sage leaf
1 small jalapeño, stem and seeds removed, diced
salt, to taste

FOR THE GARNISH
½ lime cut into wedges
⅓ cup cilantro leaves
⅓ cup chopped chives
½ cup crumbled queso fresco (optional)
⅓ cup sour cream (optional)

Use a knife to cut the kernels off the corn. Save the cobs and set kernels aside.

In a large pot, heat olive oil over medium-high heat. Add onion and garlic and cook until slightly browned, about 3 minutes. Add 8 cups of water and bring to a boil. Add cobs and reduce heat to a simmer. Cook for 30 minutes. Remove cobs from the broth and discard.

While broth is cooking, shred the petals of the zucchini flowers. Reserve ¼ of the flowers for garnish.

Add corn, potato and herbs to broth and bring it back to a boil. Reduce heat to a simmer and cook for 10 minutes or until potato is tender. Add jalapeño and petals and cook for 1 minute. Turn off heat and allow soup to cool for about 15 minutes. Pour mixture into a blender and process until just smooth. Pour puree back into the large pot. Bring to a boil. Ladle soup into bowls and garnish with lime, cilantro, chives and flower petals. If you want, sprinkle in some queso fresco and a small spoonful of sour cream.

COOK'S NOTES

No zucchini blossoms? Dice a small zucchini and add when the corn and potato go in. This soup can be totally vegan if served without the queso fresco and sour cream, but if you want to enrich it, add about ¼ cup of cream after the soup has been pureed and you are heating it up before service.

WHEAT BLINIS WITH COWBOY CAVIAR

SERVES 8 TO 12

Wheat blinis can be topped with real caviar. In Montana, Paddlefish caviar is harvested from prehistoric-looking fish from the Yellowstone River in Glendive. Paddlefish season occurs from the middle of May through June. The Glendive Chamber of Commerce and Agriculture offers free fish cleaning in exchange for harvesting roe. The donated roe is made into caviar by Yellowstone Caviar, with proceeds from sales used toward the enhancement of eastern Montana fisheries.

Roe is a delicacy and not easy to come by. For me, the next best Montana topping is bacon partnered with black beluga lentils from Timeless Natural Food. The tiny black lentils give the illusion of fish eggs, while bacon holds that essence of eating heartily in the outdoors with its saltiness and smokiness.

Wheat Blinis

Cowboy Caviar

8 ounces crème fraîche

Place blini on a platter. Put caviar into a bowl and set on platter. Scoop crème fraîche into a small bowl and place on platter next to caviar. Enjoy with crème fraîche spread on blini and topped with caviar.

WHEAT BLINIS

MAKES ABOUT 4 DOZEN

2¼ teaspoons active dry yeast (one ¼-ounce envelope)
½ teaspoon sugar
½ cup warm water (between 105°F to 110°F)
½ cup all-purpose flour
⅓ cup wheat flour
1 teaspoon baking powder
1 teaspoon salt
½ cup buttermilk
1 tablespoon unsalted butter, melted
2 large eggs, separated

Sprinkle yeast and sugar over the water. Let stand until foamy, about 5 minutes. In a medium bowl, stir together flours, baking powder and salt. In a large bowl, stir together buttermilk, butter and egg yolks. Whisk in yeast mixture followed by the flour mixture. Let stand, covered, in a warm place for 30 minutes.

Beat egg whites until stiff peaks form. Fold into batter. Let stand for 10 minutes.

Heat a large nonstick skillet over medium heat and coat with a thin layer of butter. Scoop a generous tablespoon of batter onto pan and cook until bubbles develop on the cake, about 2 minutes per side. Cool on tray.

COWBOY CAVIAR

MAKES ABOUT 1 ½ CUPS

½ pound bacon, diced
1 cup **Black Beluga Lentils**
1 tablespoon extra virgin olive oil
1 tablespoon water
2 tablespoons thinly sliced chives
fresh ground black pepper, to taste

FOR THE GARNISH
sour cream or crème fraîche
chopped hard boiled eggs

Over medium heat, in a skillet, cook bacon until browned and crispy, about 5 to 7 minutes. Scoop bits onto a paper towel to drain. (Save bacon fat from the pan for use in another recipe.)

Pour half the lentils into a medium bowl. Add olive oil and water and coarsely mash with a fork. Stir in remaining lentils, bacon bits, chives and black pepper. Serve on **Wheat Blinis**. Garnish with sour cream and hard-boiled eggs.

BLACK BELUGA LENTILS

MAKES ABOUT 3 CUPS

1 cup dried black beluga lentils

Pour lentils into a colander and remove any foreign material. Rinse and drain. Put lentils into a medium saucepan and add 2½ cups water. Bring to a boil and reduce heat to a simmer. Cook for 15 to 25 minutes, depending on desired tenderness. Drain lentils in a colander. Keep in refrigerator for up to a week.

SPINACH PICI PASTA NOODLE SOUP

MAKES 4 SERVINGS

The bright green noodles contrast beautifully with the red peppers and tomatoes in this recipe. The pasta water from boiling the noodles makes the broth base for this soup. This is one of those recipes I encourage you to be creative with; for added fun, make these with friends. Add cooked sausage or shredded roast chicken to the soup before adding the vegetables. Or omit the cheese to make the dish vegan. Fresh herbs can be substituted for the dry—just add triple the amount.

6 ounces spinach leaves

4 stalks of green onions (about 1 ounce)

1½ cups all-purpose flour (8 ounces)

8 cups of water

1 tablespoon extra virgin olive oil

1½ teaspoons salt

1 small zucchini, cut into rounds

1 red pepper, stem and seeds removed, cut into large dice

2 cloves garlic, thinly sliced

1 teaspoon dried basil leaves

1 teaspoon dried oregano leaves

1 cup cherry tomatoes, halved

FOR THE GARNISH

grated Parmigiano-Reggiano

fresh basil leaves

Line several trays with parchment paper. Set aside.

In a food processor, process the spinach and green onions until just finely chopped. Add flour and process until dough forms into a ball. The dough should not be sticky. Add more flour if necessary. Cut dough into 4 pieces. Flatten one piece of dough and, with a rolling pin, roll into a large rectangle about ¼ inch thick. Cut off a ½-inch ribbon. Fold in half lengthwise and then roll with fingers to make a thick noodle, about ¼ inch in diameter. (Note: Noodle length can be as long as you want, but 8 inches is most manageable for rolling and eating.) Place on tray, making sure noodles do not touch. Finish making noodles with the rest of dough. (The noodles can be dried or cooked right away.)

Bring water, olive oil and salt to a boil. Cook fresh noodles for 2 minutes or dried noodles for about 8 minutes or until just tender. Remove noodles with a large slotted spoon and reserve in a colander. Finish cooking all the noodles.

Bring noodle liquid back to a boil. Add zucchini, red pepper, garlic, basil and oregano to liquid. Reduce heat to a simmer and cook for 4 minutes. Bring soup back to a boil. Add noodles and cook for another minute. Add tomatoes and cook for 1 minute.

Ladle soup with vegetables and noodles into bowls. Garnish with cheese and basil. Serve immediately.

FLAVORS UNDER THE BIG SKY

BUTTER LETTUCE SALAD

MAKES 4 SERVINGS

The butter lettuce grown at Swanky Roots just outside Billings inspired this recipe. Its lettuce is so tender and delicious that only a very basic dressing is needed to flavor the leaves. Veronnaka Evenson and Ronna Klamert grow lettuce, sprouts and other greens in an aquaponics system housed in a thirty-thousand-square-foot greenhouse. Their operation allows for the tastes of spring and summer year-round, even in the dead of winter. I often grab some edible flowers or sprouts—beet, chive or broccoli—when I am at Swanky Roots and sprinkle them on this salad.

FOR THE DRESSING
2 tablespoons rice wine vinegar
3 tablespoons extra virgin olive oil
½ teaspoon Dijon mustard
½ teaspoon salt

8 ounces butter lettuce leaves
fresh ground black pepper,
  to taste

In a large bowl, whisk together dressing ingredients. Add lettuce and toss with dressing. Add pepper to taste and toss. Serve immediately.

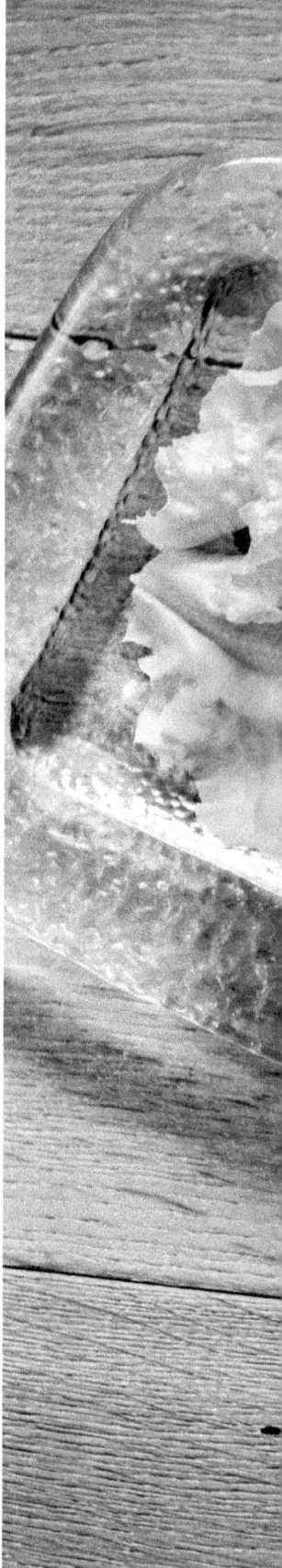

HARVESTED & COLLECTED

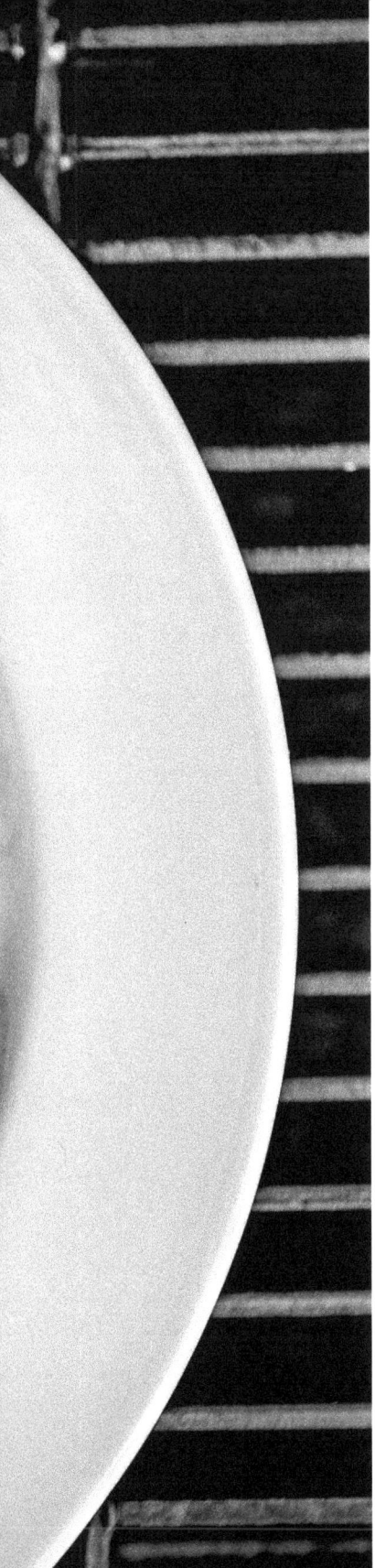

CHERRY TOMATO PESTO SALAD WITH PEACHES AND MOZZARELLA

SERVES 4 TO 6

During the summer, tomatoes and basil are the perfect partners in all things delicious. As these two come into season, peaches are also in their prime. The combination is magic. Feel free to substitute nectarines, blackberries or cherries for the peaches in this salad. The dressing can also be tossed with lettuce, arugula or even apple slices. Summer abounds with produce, so bring it all into this salad bowl.

FOR THE DRESSING
2 tablespoons **Basil Pesto**
2 tablespoons white vinegar
3 tablespoons extra virgin olive oil
1 teaspoon honey
salt, to taste

10 ounces cherry tomatoes, halved
2 peaches, peeled, cut into 1-inch chunks
6 ounces fresh baby mozzarella cheese balls (*bocconcini* or *ciliegine*), drained
1 bunch fresh basil leaves, about 20 leaves
½ cup shaved Parmigiano-Reggiano

In a small bowl, combine dressing ingredients. Place tomatoes, peaches and mozzarella on a large plate. Drizzle with dressing. Garnish with basil leaves and cheese. Serve immediately.

GREEN BEAN SALAD WITH CHICKPEAS AND BROWN MUSHROOMS

SERVES 4

For this recipe, I love using Timeless Natural Food's Black Butte Chickpeas. Typical blond chickpeas work well in this recipe, but the color contrast of the black variety is spectacular with the green beans and brown mushrooms. The dish looks earthy and inviting. I recommend using haricot verts for the green beans, as they are shorter, thinner and more tender than the Blue Lake variety. If your **Preserved Lemons** *are not ready to use, use 1 teaspoon of minced zest from a fresh lemon and a sprinkle of salt to taste. If you can get a Meyer lemon, use this lovely citrus fruit with essences of lemon, grapefruit and orange. The recipe suggests mincing the preserved lemons, but they get so soft that you can almost mash them. After pulling the lemon out of the jar, rinse quickly under some water. Use both the skin and the pulp, making sure you get rid of any seeds. You can also use capers in place of preserved lemons.*

½ pound green beans, stems trimmed

FOR THE DRESSING

2 teaspoons minced **Preserved Lemons**

¼ cup extra virgin olive oil

2 tablespoons lemon juice

½ teaspoon soy sauce

salt, to taste

4 ounces brown mushrooms, cleaned, trimmed and thinly sliced

1 cup **Black Chickpeas** or canned chickpeas, drained and rinsed

¼ cup chopped chives

2 teaspoons chopped tarragon

Steam or blanch the green beans for 4 minutes, then cool in a bowl of ice water. Drain and cut into 1-inch pieces and set aside. In a small bowl, mix together the dressing ingredients. Set aside.

In a salad bowl, combine the mushrooms, chickpeas, chives, tarragon and dressing. Let sit in the refrigerator for at least 1 hour and up to 1 day to meld the flavors. Just before service, toss in the green beans so they keep their beautiful green color.

BLACK CHICKPEAS

MAKES ABOUT 2 CUPS

1 cup Black Butte Chick Peas

In a medium bowl, add chickpeas and remove any foreign material. Add enough water to cover about 1-inch above the top of the peas. Soak overnight. Drain. Put chickpeas into a medium saucepan and add 2½ cups of water. Bring to a boil and reduce heat to a simmer. Add more water if necessary. Cook 1 to 1½ hours depending on desired tenderness. Drain chickpeas in a colander. Keep in refrigerator for up to 1 week.

SHAVED KOHLRABI WITH APPLE AND PECANS

SERVES 4 TO 6

Kohlrabi, or stem turnip, is a light-green or purple bulbous vegetable about the size of a large fist, with thick skin and leaf stems sticking out of its side. For those who do not know the vegetable, it is a source of curiosity and conversation when found at the Yellowstone Farmers' Market because it looks weird. On the inside, its texture is smooth and dense like the center of a broccoli or cauliflower stem, with flavors of cabbage, broccoli and radish. Although this salad could be made with just apple slices alone, the kohlrabi adds a delicious crunch and complements the apple beautifully.

FOR THE DRESSING

2 tablespoons cider vinegar

3 tablespoons mayonnaise

2 teaspoons honey

½ teaspoon salt or to taste

2 tablespoons capers, coarsely chopped

1 pound kohlrabi, peeled, quartered, thinly sliced on a mandoline

1 Granny Smith apple, peeled, cored, thinly sliced on a mandoline

4 green onions, thinly sliced

½ cup pecans, coarsely chopped

fresh ground black pepper, to taste

In a small bowl, mix together dressing ingredients. Set aside. In a large bowl, add kohlrabi, apple, green onion and pecans. Toss with dressing. Let sit at room temperature for 5 minutes to meld flavors. Season with black pepper and serve.

COOK'S NOTES

How to handle a kohlrabi? Take a knife and cut off the stems. Then remove the thick outer skin with a paring knife or a very sharp vegetable peeler. Cut the kohlrabi in half or in quarters before shaving into thin slices on a mandoline. Save the stems in the refrigerator for up to one week to be used in a stir-fry such as the **Pheasant Stir-Fry with Black Bean Sauce.** Cut the stem into ½-inch pieces to be added in addition or in place of the red pepper in the recipe.

RAW KALE SALAD

MAKES ABOUT 5 CUPS

With this recipe, you need to roll up your sleeves and use your hands for the best results. Massaging the kale with your fingers will soften the tough leaves and rub in the flavors of the dressing. This salad may just convert a kale skeptic into eating this nutritious green. Add some golden raisins or dried cherries for a sweet touch or sliced kalamata olives for added saltiness.

- 1 bunch (about 9 ounces with ribs) kale (preferably lacinato), ribs removed and discarded
- 1 clove garlic, peeled
- ½ teaspoon kosher salt
- 1 tablespoon extra virgin olive oil
- 1 tablespoon lemon juice
- 1 stalk green onion, thinly sliced
- ⅓ cup fresh grated Parmigiano-Reggiano

Slice the kale into ¼-inch thin ribbons. Leave on cutting board. Set aside.

Smash garlic on cutting board. Sprinkle salt on top and leave for about 3 minutes. With the knife blade, carefully mash garlic into a paste. Mince garlic with knife, if necessary.

Add garlic paste, olive oil and lemon juice to a large bowl. Add kale and, using your hands, massage the kale for 3 minutes until the kale softens. Add the green onion and grated cheese and toss with kale. Serve immediately or store in an airtight container in the refrigerator, keeping up to 3 days.

ROASTED RADISHES WITH BLUEBERRIES AND PRESERVED LEMONS

SERVES 4 TO 6

In the spring, radishes are the first colorful bounty to be harvested from the garden. But they are also available at the grocery year-round. Mostly we eat them raw, but they are unexpectedly delicious when grilled. In this recipe, I specify using blueberries, but raspberries or strawberries would be fabulous substitutes. The sweet fruit balances out the spicy, slightly bitter radishes.

1½ pounds radishes, with some stems and leaves, halved
2 tablespoons extra virgin olive oil
salt, to taste

FOR THE DRESSING
2 tablespoons minced **Preserved Lemons**
2 tablespoons lemon juice
3 tablespoons olive oil
1 teaspoon honey

½ white onion, thinly sliced
6 green onions, cut into diagonal slices
1 cup blueberries
2 tablespoons grated lemon zest

In a medium bowl, toss radishes with oil and salt. Heat barbecue grill to high. Cook radishes in a grill pan. Grill until radishes are slightly charred and tender, about 25 minutes. Let cool to room temperature. In a small bowl, combine dressing ingredients. In a medium bowl, toss radishes, onion, blueberries and zest together.

GREEN LENTILS WITH GRILLED NECTARINES AND ARUGULA, FETA AND MINT

SERVES 4 TO 6

This recipe is inspired by Claudia Krevat of Claudia's Mesa in Bozeman. This maven of legumes, who received a community grant from the Red Ants Pants Foundation in 2016 to educate home cooks and food service workers in Montanan about lentils, created an al fresco feast at her summertime Barefoot in the Parks dinner. Krevat's Colombian heritage influences the food she makes. Her food is full of spice and freshness and flavored with gusto and color in keeping with her outgoing personality. Krevat works closely with Timeless Natural Food, which sells organic legumes and grains grown in Montana.

Feel free to substitute peaches, pears or apples for the nectarines. I love the grill marks and caramelized flavors, but you could easily just add the fruit uncooked. Also, an underripe nectarine adds a satisfying crunch to the recipe.

FOR THE NECTARINES

2 nectarines, quartered

2 tablespoons extra virgin olive oil

generous pinch of salt

FOR THE DRESSING

⅓ cup fresh mint leaves

⅓ cup arugula leaves

¼ cup lime juice

2 garlic cloves

2 tablespoons honey

1 teaspoon salt

½ teaspoon cayenne pepper

⅓ cup extra virgin olive oil

FOR THE SALAD

2 cups **Green Lentils**

⅓ cup sliced green onions or chopped chives

2 cups arugula

⅓ cup crumbled feta cheese

Heat grill to high. In a bowl, toss together nectarines with olive oil and salt. Place nectarines on the grill flesh side down. Cook until grill marks form, about 3 to 5 minutes. Allow nectarines to cool. Cut quarters into 4 slices. Line the outside of a platter with the fruit. Set aside.

Into a blender, add dressing ingredients. Blend until mint, arugula and garlic are finely chopped. Set aside.

In a large bowl, add lentils, green onions and arugula. Toss with just enough dressing to coat lentils and greens, about half. Place mixture in the center of the ring of nectarines. Drizzle nectarines with remaining dressing. Garnish with cheese. Serve at room temperature or chilled.

GREEN LENTILS

MAKES ABOUT 3 CUPS

1 cup dried green lentils	Pour lentils into a colander and remove any foreign material. Rinse and drain. Put lentils into a medium saucepan and add 2½ cups water. Bring to a boil and reduce heat to a simmer. Cook for 20 to 30 minutes depending on desired tenderness. Drain lentils in a colander. Rinse in cold water, if desired. Drain thoroughly. Keep in refrigerator for up to a week.

GRILLED CORN WITH CILANTRO LIME BUTTER SAUCE

SERVES 8

There is nothing better than fresh corn on the cob, and when grilled and embellished with butter and decorated with lime, spice, cheese and herbs, I can only smile from my stomach to my soul. The grilling and the adornments elevate ordinary corn, which is already delectable, onto another level of deliciousness.

2 tablespoons plus 2 tablespoons melted butter, divided
½ teaspoon minced lime zest, divided
¼ teaspoon paprika
¼ teaspoon cayenne
½ teaspoon salt
8 ears corn, shucked, halved
salt, to taste
fresh ground pepper, to taste
⅓ cup sour cream
¼ cup chopped cilantro
¼ cup sliced green onions
⅓ cup cotija cheese
1 lime cut into wedges

Heat grill to medium high.

In a small bowl, mix together 2 tablespoons butter, lime zest, paprika, cayenne and salt. Keep warm to keep butter melted. Set aside.

Brush corn with remaining butter. Season with salt and black pepper, to taste. Place corn on grill and cover. Cook for 10 to 12 minutes, turning halfway through until corn is tender and slightly charred.

Place corn on a platter, brush with butter-lime mixture and drizzle with sour cream. Garnish with cilantro, green onions and cheese. Serve with lime wedges on the side. Enjoy immediately.

CREAMY GOAT CHEESE POLENTA

SERVES 4 TO 8

Polenta speaks ultimate comfort to me. This dish goes well with a steak for dinner or for breakfast with bacon and a fried egg sunny side up so the yolk can ooze into the polenta. Cook polenta to the consistency you like. Thick polenta can be molded into a baking dish and then sliced. Thinner, runny polenta can almost be a sauce for shrimp or steak. Then, plain polenta, sans corn and cheese and substituting in butter for olive oil, can be eaten with crème fraiche, honey and fresh berries. Vary the cheese in this dish using cheddar or smoked gouda as nice variations or, one of my favorites, fresh mozzarella. If you do choose goat cheese, I recommend Amaltheia Cheese, made in Belgrade.

2 ears corn, husks and silk removed
2 tablespoons olive oil, divided
4 cups vegetable or chicken broth
1 cup water with extra, additional 1 cup or more
salt, to taste
1 ¼ cups polenta
4 ounces fresh goat or feta cheese, crumbled
fresh ground black pepper, to taste

With a serrated knife, cut off the kernels from cob. Save the cobs and set aside. Coarsely chop the kernels and set aside.

In a large pot, heat 1 tablespoon olive oil over medium-high heat, add corn and cook for 2 to 3 minutes until kernels are slightly browned. Scoop kernels out into a bowl and set aside.

In the same pot, add broth and 1 cup water and bring to a boil. Add olive oil and salt. Pour in the polenta in a thin stream while whisking. Reduce the heat to a simmer. Cook for 20 minutes or to desired doneness, stirring often. Add a little more water if necessary as polenta cooks and becomes too thick. Stir in the cooked corn and cook for 2 minutes. Whisk in the cheese and black pepper to taste. (Note: The fresh goat cheese will melt more readily and mix into the polenta than the feta.) Serve immediately.

BEEF AND BACON STEW

MAKES 4 TO 6 SERVINGS

This is a thick stew that explodes with umami. The secret ingredient is the vibrant Barbera, made by Clint Peck at Yellowstone Cellars and Winery. The medium-bodied red wine is rich with cherry, raspberry and blackberry flavors, meaty notes, smokiness and good acidity. Peck procures his wine grapes from Washington, where he makes many trips during harvest.

I chose this wine for the recipe while in the winery's tasting room with my friend Renee Coppock, a lover of red wine and a great cook. We discussed the wine for this recipe in depth with several other guests at the bar. The vote for Barbera was unanimous. I think Clint's Dolcetto would also work. Both grapes beckon from the Piedmont region in Northern Italy. Dolcetto grapes ripen earlier, and the name means "little sweet one" in Italian. Clint's Dolcetto from Washington State is deep purple, with essences of blackberry, plum and spice, which gives the stew a more masculine anchor.

½ pound bacon, cut crosswise into 1-inch slices

1 large red onion, diced

salt, to taste

8 ounces white mushrooms, cleaned and sliced

4 garlic cloves, crushed

⅓ cup flour

1 teaspoon salt

fresh ground black pepper, to taste

2 pounds boneless beef chuck roast, cut into 2-inch cubes

extra vegetable oil, if needed

1 bottle 750ml dry red wine (Yellowstone Cellars and Winery's Barbera is ideal)

1½ tablespoons beef base

3 large carrots, cut crosswise into 1-inch pieces

salt, to taste

fresh ground black pepper, to taste

Lay out bacon pieces in a large Dutch oven without overlapping. Cook over medium heat. Turn the pieces as needed until they reach desired crispness, 8 to 12 minutes. Using a slotted spoon, transfer bacon to a large bowl. Pour most of the grease into a small bowl, leaving about 1 tablespoon in the pot.

Heat bacon fat in Dutch oven over medium-high heat, adding onions. Sprinkle with salt and stir. Cook onions without stirring for a minute until browning starts. Stir onions again, cook for 1 to 2 minutes. Stir onions again, cook 1 to 2 minutes and stir again. Add mushrooms, cook and stir for 1 to 2 minutes. Stir in garlic and cook, stirring, for 30 seconds. Remove this fragrant mixture to the bowl with bacon.

Combine flour, salt and black pepper in a medium bowl. Toss beef cubes in flour mixture to coat well. Heat 1 tablespoon bacon grease in Dutch oven. Add beef a few pieces at a time; do not let pieces touch. Cook beef cubes, undisturbed, until

nicely browned on each side, turning pieces only when browned, about 5 to 8 minutes. Repeat with remaining beef, using remaining bacon fat, or vegetable oil if necessary.

Pour bottle of red wine into the Dutch oven. Stir in beef base. Return beef, bacon, onions, mushrooms and garlic to pan; bring to a boil and reduce to a slow simmer.

Cover and cook for 1½ hours or until beef is very tender. Add carrots and simmer, covered, for 15 minutes. Season with salt and pepper to taste; stir in parsley. Serve in shallow bowls with your best mashed potatoes, buttered noodles or hot rice.

> **COOK'S NOTES**
>
> For a good-tasting stew, choose a bottle of wine you enjoy drinking. This stew is still good if you pour yourself a glass of wine while you cook the stew.
>
> Take the bacon out of the refrigerator about 15 minutes before cooking. Slightly warmer bacon cooks more easily than when it is stone cold.
>
> No beef base? Two bouillon cubes can be substituted, but keep in mind that these packets of concentrated beef broth can be salty. A few cans of beef broth, or about 4 cups, can be added to the stew instead, but keep the lid off for the long cooking. Just keep an eye on the stew, as it reduces by at least a quarter of the liquid you added.

BARLEY PILAF WITH GREEN BEANS, PEAS AND SAUSAGE

SERVES 4 TO 6

I have always loved barley because it is dense and chewy and so fun to eat. This dish is what I call a stove-top casserole. Basically, this is a concoction of meat, vegetables and grain, which means you, as the cook, can change it up any way you want. I use this recipe as a loose template for cooking up what I have left in my refrigerator. I always have frozen peas in the freezer, as they are convenient for adding to any dish.

I cook everything in stages to avoid overcooking any one ingredient, just as I do when making a successful Chinese stir-fry. Cook meats first, then the vegetables from hardest to softest.

I like to use Timeless Natural Food Organic Semi-Pearled Purple Prairie Barley. The Montana-grown barley is heartier and much prettier than the regular white version. The final dish, with its purple grain and green beans and peas, is lovely to look at.

This dish is delicious made with Project Meats' Italian sausage, regular or hot. Because my husband and I eat mostly vegan at home, we often substitute a plant-based Italian sausage from Beyond Meat or Field Roast for a vegan option. Also, diced red, orange or yellow peppers can be added when the green peas go in. Use your imagination, as my recipes are guidelines for your creativity.

1 cup frozen green peas

2 Italian sausage links, about 4 ounces each, meat squeezed out from casing

1 large shallot, diced

2 garlic cloves, minced

4 ounces green beans, cut into ¼-inch pieces

1 teaspoon mustard seeds

3 cups cooked barley

2 green onions, coarsely chopped

salt, to taste

fresh ground black pepper, to taste

Add peas to a small bowl. Add enough cold water to cover the top of the peas. Let sit for 10 minutes. Drain and set aside.

Heat a large skillet over medium to medium-high heat. Add sausage, shallot and garlic and cook for 5 minutes or until sausage and onions are browned. Add the green beans and cook for about 3 minutes until cooked to al dente. Add the mustard seeds, barley and peas and cook for 2 minutes to warm through. Remove from the heat, stir in the green onions and season with salt and black pepper, to taste. Serve immediately.

POTATO RICOTTA GNOCCHI

SERVES 4

*Potatoes are easy to come by, especially russets. These light and airy gnocchi are surprisingly simple to make and unbelievably dreamy to eat. I recommend sautéing gnocchi in olive oil or butter, as the outside then has a nice crispness. The browned dough reminds me of my childhood favorite, potstickers, the seared outside of which I savored more than the filling. These gnocchi are satisfying paired with **Roasted Tomato-Rhubarb Sauce**. These gnocchi hold up well to the dense, rich sauce. They are also memorable simply tossed with freshly grated parmesan cheese.*

1 pound russet potatoes, unpeeled
1 large egg, beaten
¼ cup whole-milk ricotta
⅔ cup all-purpose flour
2 teaspoons salt
extra virgin olive oil, or butter, for sautéing, if desired

Cover potatoes in a large saucepan with water to cover by 1 inch. Bring to a boil; reduce to a simmer and cover. Simmer gently for 25 to 35 minutes, or until potatoes are tender in the center when pierced with a knife.

Meanwhile, mix together egg and ricotta in a small bowl. In another bowl, mix the flour with the salt. Set aside.

Drain potatoes and carefully peel skin with a spoon, discarding skin. Rice or mash the potato flesh into a large bowl.

Add flour and egg mixtures to riced potato. Bring dough together with a spoon, scraping the sides until dough comes together; do not overmix. The dough should be soft but not sticky. Add very small amounts of flour, if necessary, if dough is overly sticky.

Line two baking sheets with parchment paper and dust lightly with flour. Place dough onto a lightly floured surface and divide dough into four equal pieces. Roll each piece to a log about ½ inch in diameter; slice into ¾-inch pieces. Use your fingertips to make an indentation in the center of each gnocchi or press the prongs of a fork into the center. Place on prepared baking sheet. Repeat with remaining dough.

Bring a large pot of salted water to a gentle boil. Gently lower about 20 gnocchi at a time into

simmering water. When the gnocchi float to the top, after about 3 to 4 minutes, transfer to a parchment-lined baking sheet with a slotted spoon. Continue cooking gnocchi in batches until they are all cooked. Serve immediately with your favorite pasta sauce or sauté by heating 2 teaspoons olive oil or butter in a large nonstick pan over medium-high heat. Cook about 2 minutes on each side until lightly browned.

> **COOK'S NOTES**
>
> If you want to make the gnocchi ahead of time (the day before or several hours before serving), you can cover loosely and refrigerate the uncooked gnocchi overnight in the refrigerator. Resume with simmering gnocchi, straight from the refrigerator, to serve the next day.

GARLIC, THYME AND SAGE BAKED CHICKEN WITH CHICKEN LIQUOR

MAKES 4 TO 6 SERVINGS

I crave chicken often. There is nothing better than a just baked chicken that oozes with juiciness, especially one that has been brined. The brine is the secret to the tenderness of this chicken. The aromas of chicken baking with garlic and herbs fill the air with swaddling comfort. There is no hurrying the cooking of a chicken, so anticipation is built. Once the chicken is at the table, we are ready to feast, to honor its gift of nourishment and deliciousness.

2 cups water

⅓ cup salt

2 tablespoons sugar

4 sprigs of fresh thyme

2 sage leaves

4 cloves garlic

about 4 cups of ice

1 3- to 5-pound chicken

Chicken Dipping Liquor

Combine water, salt, sugar, thyme, sage and garlic in a large pot over high heat. Bring to a boil. Cover and remove from heat. Let stand for 10 minutes.

Add ice to a large bowl. Pour brine over ice and stir until ice melts.

Place chicken in a large plastic bag and pour brine over chicken. Seal and refrigerate for 8 hours or overnight.

Heat oven to 425°F. Arrange oven rack so it is in the center of the oven.

Drain chicken and pat dry. Place chicken breast side up in a baking dish. Roast chicken until it is deeply browned and juices run clear when thigh is pricked with a knife or thermometer inserted into the thigh reads 165°F, about 1 hour and 15 minutes. Carefully drain juices from cavity into baking dish to make **Chicken Dipping Liquor**. Let rest for 10 minutes before carving.

CHICKEN DIPPING LIQUOR

MAKES ½ TO 1 ½ CUPS

*There's the French Dip Sandwich, so why not the Chicken Dip Sandwich, bathed in what I will call Chicken Dipping Liquor? The drippings of baked chicken and turkey are usually turned into gravy, but why? For me, there's pure luxury in dipping a piece of warm bread into a bowl of warm chicken drippings spirited with some chicken broth. The **No Knead Crusty Bread** is perfect for soaking up these chicken juices. The liquor is also delicious ladled over a bowl of steaming white rice.*

¼ cup to ½ cup or more of chicken drippings
½ to 1 cup or more of chicken broth
fresh ground black pepper, to taste

After scraping the dish that the garlic and thyme chicken was baked in, pour baked pieces, juice and fat into a saucepan. Add desired amount of broth and bring to a boil. Add black pepper to taste. Pour into a bowl and serve with warmed thick slices of bread.

NO KNEAD CRUSTY BREAD

MAKES 1 LARGE LOAF

*Baking artisan bread with a crusty outside and a moist, chewy inside could not be easier. Of course, what is even easier is to go downtown to pick up a loaf from Le Fournil, François Morin's exceptional bread bakery. But when I fail to secure a loaf from François, I make the dough Friday night to bake Saturday as a weekend treat. Nothing is more intoxicating than the aroma of baking bread. Biting into a slice of warm bread slathered with butter or dipped into a bowl of **Chicken Dipping Liquor**, I know this woman can live by bread alone.*

3 cups all-purpose flour, plus extra 3 tablespoons for dusting
1½ teaspoons salt
1 teaspoon sugar
1¼ teaspoons active dry yeast
1½ cups warm water (about 110°F)

In a large bowl, mix together flour, salt, sugar and yeast. Add warm water and stir until a wet, sticky dough forms. Cover the bowl with plastic wrap and set aside in warm place for at least 8 hours or overnight until dough rises, bubbles and flattens on top.

Place a Dutch oven with lid into a cold oven and heat to 450°F. Let it sit in oven for 15 minutes after the oven comes to temperature.

Dust a flat surface with flour. Scrape the dough out of bowl onto a floured surface. Shape the dough into a ball and place on parchment paper. Trim parchment with large lip for easy transfer. Cover with plastic wrap and allow to rest for 30 minutes.

Remove the Dutch oven from the oven and lift the lid. Carefully place the dough and parchment paper into Dutch oven. Cover with the lid and return it to oven.

Bake for 45 minutes. Remove the lid and bake an additional 10 minutes to bake the bread through. Let cool for at least 10 minutes before slicing!

FLUFFY WHEAT OATMEAL PANCAKES

MAKES 6 TO 8 CAKES

Thick and fluffy pancakes are everyone's favorites. There is just more cake to soak up the sweet elixir of the syrup and, of course, the butter. I like to dip a bite-size piece of pancake in warmed syrup. Most of the time, I just use my fingers because pancakes and Sunday mornings remind me of childhood. I also believe that food tastes better when eaten with your fingers. Make a whole batch of these to put in the freezer for enjoyment every morning. Just reheat in the toaster oven or microwave.

⅔ cup wheat flour

½ cup all-purpose flour

½ cup old-fashioned oats

3 tablespoons sugar

4 teaspoons baking powder

½ teaspoon salt

1½ cups milk

1 egg

3 tablespoons butter, melted

In a large bowl, mix together flours, oats, sugar, baking powder and salt. Add milk and egg and mix until smooth. Stir in melted butter.

Heat lightly oiled frying pan or griddle over medium-high heat. Scoop about ½ cup of batter onto the pan. Cook until bubbles form and batter is somewhat set, while golden brown on the bottom, or about 4 minutes. Flip and cook until golden brown, about 2 minutes. Serve each cake immediately, but if serving a crowd, keep cakes warm stacked on a plate in a 200°F oven.

BASIL VEGAN CHOCOLATE CAKE

SERVES 8

Chocolate and basil are an unlikely but delicious combination. Last year, I had a lot of Thai basil left in my garden from a plant I bought at the Yellowstone Valley Farmers' Market. At the end of the summer, I made several Basil Vegan Chocolate Cakes to put in the freezer. That way, I had a dessert ready at the last moment. Thaw the cake out and then dress it up with some chocolate sauce, strawberries and a dusting of powdered sugar for a rich treat.

Thai basil is used in Southeast Asian cooking for adding flavors of anise and cinnamon punctuated with some spice. The leaves are small and narrow, about the size of half an index finger, with purple stems and pink flowers. The basil goes into just about everything from salads to curries. Sweet basil is more readily available in Big Sky country and can be used in place of the Thai version.

I chose to share the vegan version of the cake because when my husband and I are eating at home, we mostly eat vegan or vegetarian. Oftentimes we joke that we are "flexitarians" or "convegans" because when we go out, we want to enjoy the gift of food someone has cooked for us or the offerings of a local restaurant. This cake is an expression of how we want to eat on a daily basis.

FOR DRY INGREDIENTS

2 cups all-purpose flour
1¾ cups sugar
¾ cup cocoa powder
2 teaspoons baking powder
1½ teaspoons baking soda
½ teaspoon ground cinnamon
½ teaspoon salt

FOR WET INGREDIENTS

⅔ cup unsweetened applesauce
¾ cup packed basil leaves, finely chopped
½ cup canola oil or coconut oil
1 cup unsweetened almond milk
2 teaspoons vanilla extract
1 tablespoon apple cider vinegar
1 cup boiling water

confectioners' sugar, for dusting, if desired

Heat oven to 350°F. Grease an 8-inch springform and line with parchment paper cut to just slightly larger than the diameter of the bottom. Set aside.

In a large bowl, mix together dry ingredients. In a medium bowl, mix together the wet ingredients.

Pour wet ingredients into dry mixture and whisk until well combined. The batter should be runny. Pour batter into the prepared pan. Bake for 1 hour to 1 hour and 15 minutes or until a toothpick inserted in the center comes out clean. Let cake cool in pan for 10 minutes before removing cake from the pan. Enjoy warm or at room temperature dusted with some powdered sugar, if desired.

COOK'S NOTES

For chopping up the basil, be sure to have a sharp knife. Stack the leaves on top of one another and roll them up together as though you were rolling up a cigar. Make thin slices and then chop finely. The other option is to use a pair of scissors to snip the leaves into fine pieces.

RHUBARB RASPBERRY POLENTA CAKE

MAKES 12 SERVINGS

This is the serious spring cake. Rhubarb and raspberries are swaddled in a dense cake, moist with sticky, chewy goodness. Rhubarb from your freezer is fine; raspberries can be replaced by crisp apples in the fall or ripe peaches come summer. To add another flavor dimension, serve this with a generous dollop of whipped cream flavored with freshly grated ginger or cinnamon.

1 tablespoon plus 1 cup unsalted butter
2 cups rhubarb, rinsed and sliced into ½-inch pieces
1 pint (6 ounces) fresh raspberries
3 tablespoons plus 1 cup sugar, divided
1 cup almond flour or meal*
¾ cup all-purpose flour
3 tablespoons coarse yellow cornmeal
1½ teaspoons baking powder
¼ teaspoon salt
3 large eggs
1 teaspoon vanilla extract
confectioners' sugar, for dusting, if desired

Heat oven to 350°F. Cut a piece of parchment paper to the size of the 9-inch springform pan. Grease pan with 1 tablespoon butter. Line bottom of pan with the parchment. Set aside.

In a medium bowl, stir together rhubarb, raspberries and 3 tablespoons sugar. Set aside.

In another medium bowl, blend well almond flour, all-purpose flour, cornmeal, baking powder and salt.

In bowl of a stand mixer, beat together 1 cup butter and 1 cup sugar until creamy, about 3 minutes. Beat in eggs, one at a time, and then vanilla until well blended. On low speed, add flour mixture just to blend. Spread batter into prepared pan. Arrange rhubarb and raspberries on top.

Bake for 1 hour and 10 minutes until fruit sinks into cake and cake is nicely browned. Test by tapping the top of the cake lightly with finger—it should spring back. If cake is browning too quickly, tent loosely with aluminum foil.

Remove from oven and allow to cool for about 10 minutes before carefully releasing cake from pan. Let cool about 20 minutes more and then use a large spatula to remove cake from bottom of pan. This cake is delicious served warm or at room temperature.

COOK'S NOTES

No almond flour on hand? Process one cup of blanched almonds in the food processor until very fine. No fresh rhubarb? Use frozen rhubarb. I store ½-inch slices in my freezer to pull out for this cake. After the rhubarb thaws, drain most of the juices before mixing with sugar.

SALTED HONEY CUSTARD PIE

MAKES ONE 9-INCH PIE

Over the years, my friend Debbie Sunberg has gifted me many a generous bottle of honey from Sunshine Apiary, her brother's bee business. I love to drizzle the "liquid sunshine" (as named by Kim Mueller, who I interviewed about raising bees for Flavors Under the Big Sky*) over yogurt in the morning or, better yet, over a slice of toast with ricotta.*

As a child, I absolutely adored custard pie. My Auntie Helen would always bring pies she bought at the Eastern Bakery in San Francisco when she visited us. She always arrived with several pink boxes tied with red string filled with barbecue pork buns, almond cookies and, my favorite, that custard pie. A slice of custard pie with its creamy goodness made me smile all over, as did Auntie Helen.

With the availability of honey in Montana, this recipe honors the memory of the custard pies from the City by the Bay but uses honey instead. With the sprinkle of salt at the end, the pie buzzes into another level of goodness.

Save the egg whites to make **Pavlova Roulade with Sour Cherry Sauce and Toasted Almonds**. *Otherwise, scrambled egg whites topped with* **Roasted Tomatillo Salsa** *is a delicious way to use up the whites.*

FOR THE CRUST

1½ cups all-purpose flour
1 tablespoon sugar
½ teaspoon salt
½ cup (1 stick) cold unsalted butter, cut into cubes
⅓ cup cold buttermilk

FOR THE FILLING

2 cups heavy cream
8 egg yolks
⅓ cup honey
1 teaspoon vanilla extract
¼ teaspoon salt
¼ teaspoon fresh ground nutmeg

FOR SERVING

sea salt flakes, as garnish

In a food processor bowl, blend together flour, sugar and salt with several pulses. Add butter and pulse until mixture has pea-sized crumbs. With processor running, drizzle in buttermilk until mixture pulls away from the bowl and forms a loose ball. Dough should be only slightly moist.

Remove dough to a very lightly floured surface and press into a disk, about 7 inches in diameter. Wrap in plastic wrap and refrigerate for at least 1 hour or overnight.

On a lightly floured surface, roll the crust to a diameter of about 12 to 13 inches, about ⅛ inch thick. Transfer to a 9-inch pie pan; trim and crimp edges as desired.

Heat oven to 375°F. Line pie shell with parchment and fill with pie weights (see Cook's Notes). Bake for 20 minutes until edges just begin to lightly brown. Remove crust from oven and remove pie weights. Allow to cool while making filling.

Reduce oven temperature to 325°F. In a medium saucepan, slowly heat the cream just until you see small bubbles around the edges and steam starts to wisp from the surface. In a large bowl, whisk together the egg yolks and honey. Slowly drizzle the hot cream into the yolk mixture, whisking well to prevent the yolks from cooking. Stir in the vanilla extract, salt and nutmeg.

Pour custard into prepared pie shell. Bake for 1 hour to 1 hour and 10 minutes until custard is set around edges but still a bit wobbly in the center. Test for doneness by inserting a paring knife into custard midway between the edge and the center—the knife should come out clean. The temperature of the pie at the center should be between 170°F and 180°F.

Remove pie from oven and cool to room temperature. Serve at room temperature, with each slice garnished with some crushed sea salt flakes. Cover and refrigerate any leftover pie.

COOK'S NOTES

Use commercial pie weights if you have them, or use about 1½ pounds of dried white beans. If you use beans, save them after blind baking the crust for the next time you need pie weights.

SWANKY ROOTS:
RONNA KLAMERT AND VERONNAKA EVENSON

I discovered Swanky Roots at the beginning of winter, when white had recently carpeted our landscape. Cold pierced into my body as I tried to shiver off the reality that summer was gone. In one week, I received two phone calls—one from Judy Peterson and the other from Greg Jahn, both raving about the greenhouse growing lettuce, herbs, edible flowers and microgreens. Although this was two years after mother-and-daughter team Ronna Klamert and Veronnaka Evenson first started their venture in 2016, I knew it was the right time for me to go buy some fresh lettuce after these two enthusiastic endorsements.

On a Saturday morning in November, my husband and I drove toward the Yellowstone River, between Billings and Laurel. After making the sharp right turn onto Story Road, we spied the large, red metal–sided greenhouse. A storefront has been set up on the east side of the thirty-thousand-square-foot building, situated on sixty acres.

After stepping into the space, the size of a large garage, a bank of windows provided viewing into the brightly lit area where rows of lettuce grew. In front of us we noticed the tanks, which we assumed housed fish. From the cooler, we pulled several heads of butter lettuce packaged in a hinged plastic container.

A door swung open from the back side of the room, and in walked Veronnaka with a smile. We paid her for the lettuce and vowed to return.

About a week later, I went back to Swanky Roots with Ken Siebert to talk to Veronnaka and her mother, Ronna. From the storefront area, we walked into an alcove, rubbing sanitizer on our hands before walking into the actual greenhouse where lettuce grew.

With the greenhouse temperature set to about seventy-three degrees, from the moment I stepped in, a sense of comfort immediately filled my being. I felt as though a light cashmere wrap had been slipped onto my shoulders. My head and lungs cleared with each inhale and exhale. I had entered the perfect spa environment, with clean air and soothing temperatures exuding luxury, in keeping with the business named "Swanky."

Swanke was Ronna's maiden name. Veronnaka explained, "A lot of people think of Swanky and they think of fun, fancier, newer type of things, and that's what we are all about."

The idea of starting Swanky Roots came from Ronna. While Veronnaka was pursuing her degree in agricultural education and plant science at Montana State University in Bozeman, she brought home some tomato plants. While growing them the traditional method in dirt and fresh air, Ronna decided that she wanted to explore another method of growing, free of splitting tomatoes and insects.

TOP Veronnaka Evenson of Swanky Roots in Billings lifting up a tray of lettuce from their aquaponics growing system.

BOTTOM Ronna Klamert and Veronnaka Evenson net some blue gill from their growing tanks where nutrients originate for growing greens.

Ronna proposed an aquaponics system that combined aquaculture, in which animals such as fish, snails, crayfish or shrimp are raised in tanks, with hydroponics, where plants are cultivated in water. At first, Veronnaka was leery of her mom's idea and shared, "I thought, whatever, it was just another one of your side projects." However, her initial uncertainty transformed to belief in a system that she thought was based in science. Using fish to naturally produce the nutrients for growing plants made sense to her.

Ronna placed individual seeds into a flat of two hundred cubes, which began the seeding process. After the seeds germinate, about a week later, the plants go into a shallow stream of water or Nutrient Film Technique for further root development. Veronnaka jokingly called this stage "preschool for the plants."

Rows of beds extended the length of the greenhouse space, with a width of six feet and a depth of a couple of feet. The youngest plants were found in the rows on the south end, while the larger greens were in the north-side rows. The first few rows on the southern side were occupied by produce such as kale, radishes, cabbage, nasturtiums and cherry tomatoes growing in clay pebbles the diameter of a nickel in size.

When Ronna handed me a radish to taste, I marveled at the rosy skin and, even more, at how no dirt clung to the roots. I eagerly popped the juicy and spicy globe into my mouth. But the tasting highlight was Veronnaka's offering of a chocolate cherry tomato that transported me to summer upon first bite.

Swanky Roots uses six times less water in its aquaponics recirculating system than if it grew its bounty in a field. The heart of the operation beats from four-foot-tall and six-foot-diameter tubs holding twelve thousand gallons of water and one thousand blue gill. Waste produced by the fish transforms into nutrients with the help of microbes. The plants, atop platforms with openings allowing the roots to grow into the water, absorb the nourishment in the circulating water. In essence, the plants filter water that is recirculated into the fish tanks, carried through the system to feed the plants and then returned to the tanks.

Ronna Klamert and Veronnaka Evenson hope to not only feed the community through the produce they grow but to also nourish our minds through an educational farm, teaching us how food comes to the table.

INFECTIOUS BUGGERS: FLORENCE DUNKEL, CHEF JOSEPH YOON AND JAMES ROLIN

I have been infected with an appetite for bugs. After producing the Bug Cookoff at Montana State University (MSU) in Bozeman and later a show on Cowboy Cricket Farms, I have intentionally brought insects into my diet. Dr. Florence Dunkel, Chef Joseph Yoon

and James Rolin have transmitted their enthusiasm and knowledge on bringing insects to the table.

I have never had a squeamish aversion to eating bugs, but most of the people I know react with disgust when I mention I had visited a cricket farm and judged a bug cookoff. I will eat just about anything, and I have my father to thank for that. He and I bonded by sharing delectable food at which others might turn up their noses. He taught me the joy of eating different things. Jellyfish salad, crab custard and fish cheeks always remind me of a dad who cooked special foods for me when I was a child. The words in our conversations were in the foods we tasted together.

During the moon festival in the fall, it was my father's sister, Auntie Wai Duck, who brought over tiny rice paddy snails steamed in garlic and black beans that I devoured. Then, though technically from the mollusk phylum and not a bug, I discovered French snails when I entered college. But how can anyone resist eating anything sautéed in butter and garlic?

Insects are consumed by 80 percent of the world. Most of us have inadvertently eaten bugs. We are not able to see every aphid in the lettuce in our salad or pick out the minute crumbs of beetles in our flour. The infestation of insects can come at all stages of food production, from the moment they grow under Mother Nature's watch to storage in our own pantry. The little buggers are everywhere!

STUDENT BUG COOKOFF COMPETITION

In the winter of 2019, I was invited by Chef Marcy Gaston, assistant teaching professor in the Hospitality Management and Culinary Arts Program, to be a judge for the Second Annual Bug Cookoff Competition at Montana State University in Bozeman. At first, I hesitated because I was not sure about eating food cooked by college students. Since I was not a great cook at that point in my life, I assumed that most students were still eating dorm food and lacked the skills to cook a real meal. With crawly bugs as an ingredient, I was certain I would experience some bad food. However, when I received an e-mail from photographer and friend Lynn Donaldson-Vermillion prodding me to join her and Chef Joseph Yoon as judges, I relented.

On a sunny Saturday morning, my husband and I drove to Bozeman from Billings. Luckily, a storm had passed through the day before, allowing for the roads to be cleared, providing for easy travel. When we arrived at Harrison Hall, we were greeted by Chef Gaston. A handful of students were already in the kitchen making sure they had the right ingredients for their recipes, while others were practicing their dishes for the competition.

Thirty-one years ago, Dr. Florence Dunkel, associate professor at MSU–Bozeman in the Plant Sciences and Plant Pathology Department of the College of Agriculture, started the Bug Buffet. What began with Dunkel presenting a simple dish of crickets sautéed in butter led to her teaching assistants cooking brownies, fritters and other specialties using insects as an ingredient, finally evolving into the MSU Culinary Services preparing a meal utilizing insects. This year, the buffet attracted more than one thousand people.

Four years ago, Dunkel expanded the Bug Buffet to include insect experts from the United States and Canada. Patrick Crowley, founder of Chapul, started the first company in the United States to launch an insect product and develop the first cricket flour. He was recruited by the College of Business as an entrepreneur resident, so while he was on campus, Dunkel invited him as the first speaker for her week of bug programs.

Over the years, Dunkel hoped to share the deliciousness of insects: "The other thing to remember is that it is not just about good nutrition, it's about environmental sustainability." "We need to reduce our carbon footprint," she continued, pointing out that raising a pound of beef requires 2,600 gallons of water, including the water necessary to raise the food for the cow. A pound of crickets only needs 1 gallon of water.

In 2019, Dunkel invited Chef Joseph Yoon from Brooklyn Bugs to help mentor the students. Yoon, who left the music business to pursue his love of cooking, started Brooklyn Bugs by hosting popup dinners. He soon became an ambassador for feasting on bugs with his multicourse meals. "Well, a big part of what I am trying to do is really demonstrate the versatility of insects and show how there are so many different ways you can utilize it so I might start with cricket gougeres." These French cheese puffs are innocuous when made with powdered crickets, which have a nutty taste. The meal might progress to a mealy worm fritter and then to a scorpion atop a wonton crisp.

Yoon kicked off the Bug Cookoff at one o'clock with encouragement and cheer. The students had an hour and a half to cook an entrée and a dessert using black ants, crickets and grasshoppers. With the flavor profiles of black ants having a lemony pop and crickets and grasshoppers having nutty essences, the students went to work.

Yoon had worked with the students the night before, and it was obvious that his consultation paid off, as the kitchen was calm. Although most had not really cooked before, everyone proceeded confidently with the making of their dishes. Most professed to finding recipes on the internet.

Maria Abbot, a liberal studies major with a minor in museum in Native American studies, knew what to expect, this being her second year of competition. With an ambitious menu of sushi, finished with ginger cupcakes, she said her goal was, "Trying to keep everything going along, and getting everything nice and pretty."

Ben Hale added humor to his dessert: "It's called a picnic salad because it has fruit and stuff in it, and then we figured you can't have a picnic without ants so we're adding these black ants to it."

As the competitors were finishing up their dishes, the fire alarm went off. At first, everyone ignored the warning, but soon we found ourselves standing outside in the cold. After about fifteen minutes, everyone returned to the kitchen to be given another half hour to complete their cooking.

Chef Yoon, Lynn and I tasted delicacies ranging from street tacos with ants to omelets with green peppers, ham and crickets; cricket dumplings; minty chocolate whoopie pies with black ants; and tuna ant sandwiches. With every dish showing attention and finesse, we finally decided on a winner. Laurel Aytes and teammates Rochelle Maderal and Kael Van Buskirk won with Cricket Potato Latkes with Applesauce and Turmeric Aioli, served with a dessert of Key Lime Meringue Pie with Blackberry Ant Reduction. The modified recipes from Lauren's mother were artistically plated and showcased good cooking, even though Lauren had never cooked the dessert before.

It was an honor to be a part of the Second Annual Bug Cookoff, as I was stung with bugalicious food. I was glad that Chef Marcy Gaston and Lynn Donaldson-Vermillion bugged me into participating. I thank Dr. Florence Dunkel for infecting all with "Bug Appétit."

COWBOY CRICKET FARMS

Dr. Dunkel's contagious enthusiasm introduced me to Cowboy Cricket Farms. I met Ken Siebert in Bozeman shortly after the Fourth of July weekend. We drove just beyond the Bozeman Yellowstone International Airport to an industrial area right under the flight pattern of the planes. We met up with James Rolin, marketing manager for Cowboy Cricket Farms.

The company started in 2016 with the Cowboy Chirp Cookie, a chocolate chip cookie made with the company's own cricket powder. The company then ventured into selling snacks of whole crickets in flavors of smoke, cinnamon, wasabi and original.

The idea for the company came from Kathy while she was attending Montana State University as a nutrition student. Kathy's husband, James, the marketing manager, credited his wife with crossing paths with Dr. Florence Dunkel. When Kathy approached James with the idea of opening a cricket farm, he said, "'No, this is a horrible, horrible idea. We're not doing this.' But as usual, she was right, I was wrong. And so, two and a half years later, here we are."

Being parents to Elise, age nine; Olive, seven; and Liam, five, the Rolins wanted to develop a product that was approachable and tasty. With James's description of a cricket tasting like "a potato chip and a sunflower seed," the taste may sound appealing, but most Americans are reluctant when it comes to eating insects.

Although the Rolins started Cowboy Cricket Farms with the actual raising of crickets, today the production effort is outsourced. They started a comprehensive, eight-part, free tutorial on "How to Farm Crickets" on YouTube. At their facility, they also offer weeklong and one-day courses. During these classes, partner farmers are trained and recruited for their Partner Farmer Program. This way, the Rolins know that their cricket supply is being raised to their standards.

Today, crickets are raised in their facility for research and development. When the Rolins are not producing for their own products, their kitchen is rented to caterers or other food developers. Otherwise, they follow their business motto of bringing "bugs to the world in fun and exciting ways."

PANTRY

SEASONINGS, SAUCES AND CONDIMENTS

This section holds the key to my flavorings and seasonings for the dishes I cook. When we first moved to Montana twenty years ago, I brought these concoctions with me from San Diego. I grew up with many of the combinations and found them perfect for cooking with the meats, fish and other bounty I found here under the Big Sky. Making my own combinations in flavorings gave me permission to customize them to my palate and to my husband's tastes. Although many of the ingredients are more available ready-made these days through online ordering and at the grocery stores, I still make my own mixtures. The seasonings, sauces and condiments are just so much more vibrant when they are made fresh.

CURRY POWDER

MAKES ABOUT ½ CUP

This is the curry powder I grew up with. Although my father used a store-purchased blend, the homemade version is so much more robust in flavor. This spice powder is not true Eastern Indian but rather a concoction created by the British. Dad, after he left China, must have come across this when he lived in Hong Kong, when it was a British colony.

When buying the premade powder at the store, you will discover that formulas vary. You do not have to toast the seeds for the recipe, but I strongly recommend it, as it brings out its true personality. Dad added this spice mixture to boxed mashed potatoes. Spread on white bread with crusts removed, I thought it was divine.

*Under Big Sky country, I use the curry powder as my secret seasoning for lamb chops and a pickup for bean soups. Of course, I made mashed potatoes, and I share my recipe inspired by Dad's in **Curry Mashed Potatoes**.*

2 tablespoons coriander seeds
1 tablespoon cumin seeds
2 teaspoons mustard seeds
1 teaspoon dried fenugreek seeds
2 dried árbol chilis, stem removed
2 tablespoons turmeric powder
1 teaspoon ginger powder

In a dry pan over medium heat, toast coriander, cumin, mustard, fenugreek seeds and chilis until just fragrant. Grind spices in a grinder until a powder forms. Stir in turmeric and ginger powders. Store in airtight container for up to 3 months.

FIVE-SPICE POWDER

MAKES ABOUT ¼ CUP

Five-spice powder is one of those very distinctive Chinese spices I grew up with. I needed this spice from my father's kitchen to be in my adult pantry in this new place I called home. When I was a child, this seasoning was literally in every savory dish. Barbecue pork, meatballs and roast duck exuded the aromas and taste of this spice combination.

Five-spice powder is not a favorite of my husband, specifically because of the star anise flavor, so in my concoction I have customized the formula. If you want more of the assertive anise component, just increase the amount in the mixture. Also, if you want a spicier, more numbing effect, just add more Sichuan peppercorns. Lightly dust this on a Montana steak with some salt and pepper, and the steak will take on a more global vibe.

1 tablespoon Sichuan peppercorns
3 star anise
1 teaspoon whole cloves
1 stick cinnamon
2 teaspoons fennel seeds

Put all ingredients in a spice or coffee grinder and grind to a fine powder. Store in an airtight container for up to several months.

COFFEE COCOA SEASONING RUB

MAKES ABOUT ⅓ CUP

Coffee and cocoa mixed with garlic and chilis immediately conjure up strength and robustness. When rubbed onto a steak—bison, beef or elk—and then grilled, the fat from the meat melds beautifully with the flavors from the seasoning. Make a batch of this rub for gifting friends to make their lives more flavorful!

2 tablespoons finely ground coffee beans
1 tablespoon dark brown sugar
1 tablespoon salt
2 teaspoons ground unsweetened cocoa powder
1 teaspoon garlic powder
1 teaspoon chipotle chili powder
½ teaspoon fresh ground black pepper

In a bowl, combine the ingredients for the seasoning rub and set aside. Keep in an airtight container at room temperature for 6 months.

> **COOK'S NOTES**
>
> For additional flavor dimensions, add 1 tablespoon powdered mustard along with 1 teaspoon of cloves and ½ teaspoon of cinnamon—or more chili powder if you want more kick.

HOMEMADE HOISIN SAUCE

MAKES ABOUT ⅔ CUP

In the savory world, hoisin sauce is my chocolate sauce. I could slather this luscious, rich concoction on toast and eat it alone. Growing up, this was why I loved roast duck when my family joined in celebration banquets. It was not as much for the duck but for the sauce and julienned green onions that were stuffed into **Mandarin Pancakes**.

COOK'S NOTES

Salt-fermented black beans are soybeans that have been dried and fermented with salt. They are the olives or capers in the Chinese world of cooking. Though not usually eaten alone, they add umami and saltiness to a dish. The beans are found at Asian grocery stores on the shelf, sold in plastic bags or in a cardboard can. When you get them home, pour them into an airtight jar; I put the bag in a storage bag. Then I bury the beans in the corner of my cheese drawer to keep the aroma contained. The beans have a rich, deep, savory aroma that can permeate a space, much like garlic cooking. The beans last indefinitely and dehydrate over time. If they are super dry, just rehydrate them in a little water. Before using the beans, do look for any debris.

½ cup dark brown sugar
¼ cup salt fermented black beans, rinsed and drained
¼ cup soy sauce
2 tablespoons balsamic vinegar
2 tablespoons apricot jam
2 teaspoons sesame oil
1 teaspoon **Five-Spice Powder**

Put all ingredients into a blender or food processor. Process until smooth. Keep in an airtight container in the refrigerator for up to 2 weeks.

BLACK BEAN SAUCE

MAKES ABOUT 1 CUP

If I was to choose a savory sauce to go on any seafood or meat dish I cook, this would be it. Salt-fermented black soy beans exude just the right amount of saltiness and umami to a dish, while garlic and ginger make the perfect seasoning pair of spice and flavor. Umami is that fifth taste after sweet, salty, sour and bitter and is associated with what is found in broths and meats. Cooked tomatoes and sautéed mushrooms also exude a good amount of umami. Although this sauce is good on top of grilled lamb or stir-fry shrimp, I am perfectly happy with it poured over a pile of egg noodles.

1 tablespoon vegetable oil
2 tablespoons salt fermented black beans, rinsed, coarsely chopped
3 cloves garlic, minced
2 teaspoons minced ginger

FOR THE SAUCE
2 tablespoons soy sauce
1 teaspoon dry sherry
½ teaspoon sugar
¾ cup chicken broth
2 teaspoons cornstarch

In a bowl, combine the sauce ingredients. Mix well. Set aside.

In a saucepan, heat oil over medium-high heat. Add black beans, garlic and ginger. Stir-fry until fragrant, about 1 minute. Then add sauce mixture. Bring to a boil and stir until sauce thickens, about 2 minutes.

THAI PEANUT DIPPING SAUCE

MAKES ABOUT 1 CUP SAUCE

This is one of those sauces that can go with just about anything. It actually could go well with the **Bison Sirloin Steaks with Coffee Cocoa Rub** *or served with the* **Roast Duck with Steamed Buns** *instead of the* **Homemade Hoisin Sauce**.

FOR THE DIP

¼ cup unsalted peanut butter
¼ cup coconut milk
¼ cup soy sauce
2 tablespoons unseasoned rice vinegar
2 tablespoons sugar
½ teaspoon hot chili oil
1 teaspoon lime juice
2 cloves garlic, minced
2 tablespoons cilantro leaves, finely chopped
1 green onion, thinly sliced

In a medium bowl, combine dip ingredients. Serve with **Roasted Eggplant**.

DUKKAH

MAKES ⅜ CUP

This is another one of those recipes where there is a ton of latitude as to what you can add. The traditional Dukkah originated in Egypt and consisted of raw hazelnuts, sunflower seeds and coriander ground up, with the addition of whole sesame seeds and cumin seeds. I simplified the recipe by using just three ingredients, with the extra step of toasting the spice, nuts and seeds to bring out their personalities. An easy way to enjoy Dukkah is to sprinkle it over bread dipped in olive oil.

- 1 tablespoon cumin seeds
- 3 tablespoons sesame seeds
- 2 tablespoons finely chopped almonds
- salt, to taste

In a cold skillet, add cumin, sesame seeds and almonds. Heat to medium and toast until cumin is fragrant and sesame seeds and almonds start to lightly brown, about 3 minutes. Scoop mixture into a small bowl. Season with salt to taste.

PICKLED CUCUMBERS AND CARROTS

MAKES ABOUT 1½ CUPS

These pickles can literally go with anything. I make them to go with the **Pork Meatballs Banh Mi Sandwiches** *with* **Homemade Hoisin Sauce**. *These veggies give a hotdog or a grilled burger that wonderful salty, sweet and sour punch.*

- 2 large carrots, peeled, julienned
- 1 cucumber, peeled, seeds removed, julienned
- 3 tablespoons sugar
- 2 tablespoons salt
- ½ cup rice wine vinegar

In a large bowl, mix together carrots and cucumber with sugar and salt. With your fingertips, massage salt and sugar into the vegetables. Add vinegar and then just enough water to cover the vegetables. Let vegetables sit in the refrigerator for at least 1 hour. Store leftovers in a jar for up to 1 week.

ROASTED TOMATO-RHUBARB SAUCE

MAKES ABOUT 2 CUPS

I make this sauce when rhubarb is taking over my garden or I have some frozen in the freezer. The sauce acquires its savory sourness from the rhubarb, but it's also good without. I often make it if I find myself with a large container of tomatoes I haven't used up. I recommend you change up flavors by adding dried chili peppers, thyme or even curry powder. Although dried herbs are recommended here, fresh are always good. Use three times the amount of fresh to dried herbs.

1½ pounds tomatoes
8 ounces rhubarb, sliced into ½-inch pieces
1 medium onion, peeled and coarsely chopped
4 cloves garlic, peeled and crushed
3 tablespoons extra virgin olive oil
2 tablespoons brown sugar
1 teaspoon dried oregano
1 teaspoon dried basil
1 teaspoon salt

Heat oven to 425°F. In a 9x13-inch baking pan, gently stir together all ingredients. Bake for 45 minutes to 1 hour, until mixture is softly bubbling and liquid has reduced to almost jam-like texture. Let sauce cool slightly before pureeing in food processor or in a hand-held food mill. Taste and adjust seasoning, as desired, for salt and pepper. Cover and refrigerate (up to 5 days) or freeze (up to 3 months).

Reheat gently to serve as desired, as with hot cooked pasta, polenta or **Potato Ricotta Gnocchi.**

RHUBARB CHUTNEY

MAKES ABOUT 3 CUPS

Sour, sweet, salty and spicy. There is no better flavor combination to wake up the taste buds. This chutney is excellent on grilled fish or lamb chops. It is also good on a piece of toast spread with ricotta or goat cheese. For an easy dip, mix some chutney with some sour cream and surround it with pita chips.

1 tablespoon canola oil
1 small onion, small diced
2 cloves garlic, minced
1 tablespoon finely chopped fresh peeled ginger
⅓ cup sugar
⅓ cup apple juice
1 tablespoon cider vinegar
salt, to taste
⅓ cup golden raisins
½ teaspoon red chili flakes
1 pound rhubarb, trimmed and sliced

Heat oil in a medium saucepan over medium heat. Cook onion until translucent, about 5 minutes. Add garlic, ginger, sugar, juice, vinegar and salt and bring to a boil. Cook for 2 minutes or until sugar dissolves. Add raisins and red chili flakes and cook for another minute. Add the rhubarb and cook until it breaks down, about 4 minutes.

COOK'S NOTES

Sample the chutney and adjust the flavoring, adding more sugar or vinegar if necessary. The chutney can be stored in the refrigerator for up to 1 week.

ROASTED TOMATILLO SALSA

MAKES ABOUT 1 CUP

When I finally discovered tomatillos at our Yellowstone Valley Farmers' Market in Billings, I was overjoyed. I grew tomatillos when we lived in San Diego. The husk acts like a wrapper for the present inside. Tomatillos remind me of green tomatoes in appearance and a bit in taste—tart and vegetal. In fact, the Spanish name translates to "little tomatoes." When the husk is removed, the sticky residue is quickly washed off with warm water. Tomatillos are usually a light spring green in color but can come in shades of purple, which lighten to a yellow-green shade when cooked.

The tomatillos can be substituted with Roma tomatoes, and if it is summer, this recipe can be made skipping the roasting step for all the vegetables. Fresh tomatoes of all varieties can be substituted for the tomatillos.

8 ounces tomatillos, about 4 medium, husks removed, halved
1 serrano or jalapeño, cut in half lengthwise, stem and seeds removed
2 cloves garlic, peeled and crushed
1 small white onion, quartered
6 sprigs cilantro, coarsely chopped
1 stalk green onion, coarsely chopped
salt, to taste

Spray a 9x13-inch baking dish with oil cooking spray. Put tomatillos, pepper, garlic and onion in prepared dish and place 4 inches below broiler. Cook until vegetables blacken in several spots, about 5 minutes. Allow vegetables to cool to room temperature.

Put vegetables into a food processor. Add cilantro and green onion. Process until everything is coarsely chopped or, if desired, more finely chopped. Scrape salsa into a serving bowl. Season to taste with salt.

CARAMELIZED ONION JAM

MAKES ABOUT 1 ¼ CUPS

*For the ultimate decadence, spread some butter on a warm piece of toasted bread and top it with this jam or stuff it into a warm croissant. It is a condiment that crosses between sweet and savory. Make sure to spread this onto the **Big Sky Bison Burger**.*

1 cup **Caramelized Onions**
2 tablespoons sugar
1 tablespoon balsamic vinegar
salt, to taste

In a saucepan, heat onions over medium heat. Add sugar, vinegar and salt. Cook until sugar melts, about 2 minutes. Cook for another 2 minutes to warm onions through.

CARAMELIZED ONION DIP

MAKES ABOUT 1 ½ CUPS

The homemade version of onion dip is far better than using the soup mix. I love making this dip to go with my most favorite chips of all time, Ruffles.

½ cup cooled **Caramelized Onions**
1 cup sour cream
1 teaspoon fresh thyme
salt, to taste
fresh ground black pepper,
 to taste

In a medium bowl, mix together onions, sour cream and thyme and season with salt and pepper to taste. Refrigerate and stir again before serving.

CARAMELIZED ONIONS

MAKES ABOUT 1 CUP

Caramelized onions are worth waiting for. Let them slowly melt as they brown. While they cook on the stove top, your house will fill with delectable aromas. I always joke that you can convince your dinner guests you have cooked all day by just caramelizing some onions. The onions are perfect spread on bread for a leftover chicken sandwich or served alongside a steak.

1 tablespoon extra virgin olive oil
2 large red onions (about 1 pound), sliced
salt, to taste

In a large skillet, heat olive oil over medium heat. Add enough onions to cover the bottom of the pan. Sauté until slightly translucent, about 2 to 3 minutes. Reduce the heat slightly if the onions are browning too much on the edges. Stir in a handful of onion and repeat cooking and stirring until all the onions have been added.

Reduce heat to medium-low and continue cooking the onions until they turn golden brown, about 15 to 20 minutes. Stir every few minutes to prevent onions from sticking to the pan or burning. If onions do start to dry out and burn, add a little water, a few tablespoons at a time. Once onions are soft and brown, remove the pan from the heat. Let the onions cool. Transfer them to an airtight container to keep in the refrigerator for up to 1 week.

PESTOS

I make pesto often. Technically, pesto alla Genovese is made up of crushed basil, garlic, Parmigiano-Reggiano, pine nuts and olive oil. However, when we first moved here years ago, basil and pine nuts were not as readily available in the local grocery stores as they are now. I started substituting spinach for basil and other nuts for the pine nuts, and I've continued to this day. As I began to substitute the real ingredients of pesto, I came up with including capers and olives and replacing the parmesan cheese with Manchego and Romano.

One of the easiest meals I make for dinner is pesto with pasta served with a side salad. Pesto can also be spread on bread, topped with some cheese and broiled, used for a dressing on a salad or dolloped on baked potatoes along with sour cream, chives and bacon.

BASIL PESTO

MAKES ABOUT 1 CUP

2 cups fresh basil leaves
⅓ cup pine nuts
3 cloves garlic
½ cup freshly grated Parmigiano-Reggiano
½ cup extra virgin olive oil
salt, to taste

Into a food processor bowl, add basil, pine nuts and garlic. Pulse several times until garlic and nuts are minced. Add cheese and pulse several times. Be sure to scrape the sides. While processor is running, add oil in a steady stream. Process until all ingredients are incorporated.

SPINACH CAPER PESTO

MAKES ABOUT 1 CUP

4 cups spinach leaves, packed
½ cup raw pistachios
2 tablespoons capers
½ cup grated Parmigiano-Reggiano
½ cup extra virgin olive oil

Into a food processor bowl, add spinach, pistachios and capers. Pulse several times until nuts are minced. Add cheese and pulse several times. Be sure to scrape the sides. While processor is running, add oil in a steady stream. Process until all ingredients are incorporated.

KALE OLIVE PESTO

MAKES ABOUT 1 CUP

4 Lacinato or Dinosaur kale leaves, stems removed, coarsely chopped
½ cup raw cashews
½ cup Castelvetrano olives
½ cup freshly grated Romano cheese
½ cup extra virgin olive oil

Into a food processor bowl, add kale, cashews and olives. Pulse several times until nuts are minced. Add cheese and pulse several times. Be sure to scrape the sides. While processor is running, add oil in a steady stream. Process until all ingredients are incorporated.

SPINACH CILANTRO LEMON PESTO

MAKES ABOUT 1 CUP

1 cup spinach leaves
1 bunch cilantro, about 4 ounces
½ preserved lemon, rinsed with water, seeds removed
½ cup walnut pieces
½ cup grated Manchego cheese
½ cup extra virgin olive oil

Into a food processor bowl, add spinach, cilantro, lemon and walnuts. Pulse several times until walnuts are minced. Add cheese and pulse several times. Be sure to scrape the sides. While processor is running, add oil in a steady stream. Process until all ingredients are incorporated.

PRESERVED LEMONS

MAKES 1 QUART JAR

I first learned of preserved lemons from my friend Kitty Morse, a cookbook author and culinary educator specializing in Moroccan cuisine. When I tasted these salted lemons for the first time, I was reminded of the salted plums I grew up with that I treasured—fruit flavor finished with saltiness. These days, I often use slices of the preserved lemon rind in place of olives or capers. They make a great base for salad dressings and are delicious used with grilled fish on a plank in the barbecue.

8 to 10 lemons (Meyers preferred)
½ cup to 1 cup kosher salt
sterilized quart canning jar
more lemon juice, if necessary

Rinse and scrub lemons clean. Juice 3 lemons and set aside. Cut off ¼ inch from the tip of the remaining lemons. Cut the lemons lengthwise in half, keeping the lemons attached at the base by not cutting all the way through. Make another cut as though quartering the lemons, again not cutting all the way through.

Put 2 tablespoons of salt into the bottom of a jar. Gently pull open the lemons and dust with salt inside and out. Press lemons into jar and press them down so the juices come out. Pack the jar with lemons, making sure they are covered with juice. If there is any lemon still showing at the top, top with some salt.

Seal the jar with the lid and let sit at room temperature for a few days. Turn the jar upside down every so often to prevent mold from forming on the lemons. After a few days, put the jar in the refrigerator for at least 3 weeks, until the rinds of the lemons soften. Turn the jar upside down occasionally while storing in the refrigerator.

To use the lemons, remove from the jar and rinse them to remove the salt. Discard the seeds and the pulp. Thinly slice or chop the preserved lemon rind.

Preserved lemons can be stored in the refrigerator for up to 1 year.

PICKLED SOUR CHERRIES

MAKES 1 QUART

In the world of sweet, sour, salty and bitter, my husband's vote would be for sour and salty above all. His love of sour and salty tastes inspired me to create these pickles from our sour cherries. In the jar with the pickling solution, they are nearly too pretty to eat, but I will sacrifice them to accompany **Smashed Potatoes with Smoked Trout***. If you do not have sour cherries, the pickling solution can be used with cucumbers, zucchini or carrots.*

1 cup water
¾ cup red wine vinegar
¾ cup sugar
2 tablespoons salt
2 teaspoons mustard seeds
2 teaspoons black peppercorns
4 dried whole red chilis such as the chile de árbol or Bird's eye chili
4 garlic cloves
½ small white onion, sliced
2 cups sour cherries with stems

In a medium saucepan, bring water, vinegar, sugar, salt, mustard seeds, peppercorns and chilis to a boil. Cook until sugar dissolves, about 2 minutes. Add garlic and onion to the bottom of the jar size you choose. Then add cherries. Pour pickling liquid over the cherries, garlic and onions. Cover and chill for 1 day.

COOK'S NOTES

I keep the pickles until I see evidence of spoilage such as mold, bubbling, slipperiness or bad odors.

SOURCES

BÉQUET CONFECTIONS
55 Caramel Court, Bozeman, Montana 59718
877.423.7838
bequetconfections.com

BROCKEL'S CHOCOLATES
117 North Twenty-Ninth Street, Billings, Montana 59101
406.248.2705
https://www.facebook.com/Brockels-Chocolates-1428931200669334/?fref=nf

COWBOY CRICKET FARMS
181 Unit 1, Skyway Boulevard, Belgrade, Montana 59714
406.209.5999
cowboycricket.com

4TH AVENUE MEAT MARKET
117 North Twenty-Fifth Street, Billings, Montana 59101
406.252.5686
4thavenuemeat.com

IGLOBALFOOD
13813 Foulger Square, Woodbridge, Virginia 22192
iGlobalFood.com

SOURCES

LE FOURNIL
2805 First Avenue North, Billings, Montana 59101
406.850.8586

MOUNTAIN ROSE HERBS
PO Box 50220, Eugene, Oregon 97405
800.879.3337 or 541.741.7307
mountainroseherbs.com

RANCH HOUSE MEAT COMPANY
3203 Henesta Drive, Billings, Montana 59102
406.656.0777
ranchhousemeatco.biz

SEAFOODS OF THE WORLD
5800 Interstate Avenue, Billings, Montana 59101
406.534.8712
seafoodsoftheworld.com

SWANKY ROOTS
8333 Story Road, Billings, Montana 59101
406.656.7668
swankyroots.com

TIMELESS NATURAL FOODS
48 Ulm-Vaughn Road, Ulm, Montana 59485
406.866.3340
timelessfood.com

YELLOWSTONE CELLARS AND WINERY
1335 Holiday Circle, Billings, Montana 59101
406.281.8400
yellowstonecellars.com

INDEX

A

Abbot, Maria 189
American Fork Ranch 16, 108
apples
    Brown Butter Five-Spice Apple Tart 36
arugula
    Green Lentils with Grilled Nectarines and Argula, Feta and Mint 162
asparagus
    Asparagus, Radish and Cherry Salad 62
    Asparagus Tortilla 73, 74
    James Honaker's Morel Mushroom Sherry Thyme Cream Sauce Pasta 70
    Roasted Asparagus 74
Aytes, Laurel 189

B

barley
    Barley Pilaf with Green Beans, Peas and Sausage 171
    Sweet Rice and Barley Coconut Pudding 50
Barngrover, Jim 16
Barta, Bud 16
basil
    Basil Pesto 153, 208
    Basil Vegan Chocolate Cake 178
Baskin, Bill 17
Baukema, Veronika 17
beef
    Beef and Bacon Stew 168
    Grilled Flank Steak with Asian Chimichurri Sauce 42
    Korean Beef 28, 41
beets 121
    Beets, Olives, Mint and Dukkah Salad with Orange Vinaigrette 130
    Roasted Beet Pesto 131
    Roasted Beets 131
Béquet Confections 16, 36, 53, 56
Béquet, Robin 16, 56, 58
Beringer's Winery 82
bison 22, 124, 126, 198
    Big Sky Bison Burger with Blue Cheese, Caramelized Onions and Bacon 124, 206
    Bison Sirloin Steaks with Coffee Cocoa Rub 126, 201
Bland, Wiley and Marilyn 34, 84

blueberries
  Roasted Radishes with Blueberries and Preserved Lemons 161
Boogman, Jan and Judy 55, 56
Bridge Creek Back Country and Wine Bar 53
Brittingham, Aaron 109
Brockel, Gary 17, 56
Brockel, Jaci 56
Brockel, Jodi 17, 56
Brockel's Chocolates 17, 56, 80
Buffalo Block at The Rex 118
Bug Cookoff 16, 186, 187, 188, 189
Burgad, Gene 108, 113, 117, 118, 119
Burghoff, Gena 53

C

Canary, Martha Jane "Calamity Jane" 113
Caramel Cookie Waffles 56
Carbon Fork 53, 109
carrots 47, 133, 134, 135, 168, 169, 202, 212
  Asian Carrot Slaw 135
  Cold Carrot Ginger Soup 47, **134**
  Pickled Cucumbers and Carrots 47, 202
  Roasted Carrots with Turmeric and Coriander 134
  Whole Roasted Carrots 133, 134
Carter's Brewing 17, 53
chanterelle mushrooms 95, 96
  Chanterelle Risotto 95
cherries
  Asparagus, Radish and Cherry Salad 62
  Pavlova Roulade with Sour Cherry Sauce and Toasted Almonds 76, 182
  Pickled Sour Cherries 212
  Sparkling Cherry Sangria 75
chicken 17, 26, 34, 56, 70, 97, 140, 148, 166, 174, 175, 200, 207
  Chicken Dipping Liquor 174, **175**, 176
  Garlic, Thyme and Sage Baked Chicken with Chicken Liquor 28, **174**
chickpeas 16, 56, 121, 154, 155
  Black Chickpeas 154, **155**
  Green Bean Salad with Chickpeas and Brown Mushrooms 154
Chico Hot Springs 17, 30
Chimichurri Sauce 42
chokecherries 128
  Linzer Cookies with Chokecherry Jam 128
coconut 50, 51, 178, 201
  Sweet Rice and Barley Coconut Pudding 50
Cody, Buffalo Bill 113, 118
coffee 53, 80, 197, 198
  Coffee Cocoa Seasoning Rub 126, **198**
corn 42, 89, 121, 142, 143, 165, 166
  Creamy Goat Cheese Polenta 166
  Grilled Corn with Cilantro Lime Butter Sauce 165
  Zucchini Flower Corn Soup 142
Cowboy Cricket Farms 16, 53, 80, 186, 189, 191
crickets 52, 56, 80, 188, 189, 191, 192
  Prairie Surprise Cowboy Cookies 80
Crowley, Patrick 188
Curry Powder 18, 44, 46, **196**, 203

D

Davis, Kevin 118
Dawood, Andleeb 17
Drage, Joshua 17, 30
duck 18, 22, 26, 197, 199
  Roast Duck with Steamed Buns 26, 28, 201
Duenow, Krissy 113, 117, 118
Dunkel, Florence, Dr. 16, 186, 188, 189, 191

E

eggplant
    Baba Ghanoush 136
    Roasted Eggplant 136, **137**, 201
eggs 18, 67, 73, 80, 100, 122, 144, 146, 147, 180
    Asparagus Tortilla 73, 74
    Chive Dutch Baby 65, 67, **122**
    Salted Honey Custard Pie 182
elk
    Elk Kielbasa with Pomegranate 91
    Pan Seared Elk Fajitas 88
Engebretson, Jeremy 17
Erickson, Kay 13
Erickson, Mike 110
Evenson, Veronnaka 16, 150, 184, 185, 186

F

Fancy Sushi Asian Fusion 17
fermented black beans 199
    Black Bean Sauce 34, 88, 157, **200**
    Homemade Hoisin Sauce 26, 28, 34, 44, 47, 92, **199**, 201, 202
Five-Spice Powder 26, 36, 49, **197**, 199
Fleur de Sel 84
flour
    Fluffy Wheat Oatmeal Pancakes 177
    Mandarin Pancakes 26, 92, **94**, 199
    No Knead Crusty Bread 175, **176**
    Steamed Buns 28
    Wheat Blinis 144, **146**
    Wheat Blinis with Cowboy Caviar 144
Flowers, Shane and Tanya 16, 108, 110, 111, 112
Fong, Chor Man 18
Fong, Man Kin 18
Franklin, Ross 41

G

Gallatin River Lodge 17, 30
Gaston, Marcy 187, 188, 189
Gayvert, Shelli 16
Gerard's Brasserie 82
Gochujang 41
gooseberries 97
    Roast Pork Chops with Grapes, Gooseberries and Rosemary 97
grapes
    Roast Pork Chops with Grapes, Gooseberries and Rosemary 97
green beans
    Barley Pilaf with Green Beans, Peas and Sausage 171
    Green Bean Salad with Chickpeas and Brown Mushrooms 154
Guillas, Bernard 118

H

Hale, Ben 189
Hart, Senia 113
Hastings, Tom 16
Hauptman, Tom and Kim 88
Heimer, H. Alfred 113
hoisin sauce
    Homemade Hoisin Sauce 26, 28, 34, 44, 47, 92, **199**, 201, 202
Honaker, James 17, 70, 82, 83, 84, 85
honey
    Salted Honey Custard Pie 182
Hospitality Management and Culinary Arts Program 187
huckleberries 87, 106
    Huckleberry Lemon Pudding Cake 106
    Pork Tenderloin with Huckleberry Hoisin Ginger Glaze 92

INDEX

J

James Beard Foundation 10, 17, 53, 82
James, Will 113

K

kale 122, 158, 186, 210
    Kale Olive Pesto 210
    Raw Kale Salad 158
Kate's Garden 16
KettleHouse Brewing Company 17
Klamert, Ronna 16, 150, 184, 185, 186
kohlrabi 157
    Shaved Kohlrabi with Apple and Pecans 157
Krevat, Claudia 16, 56, 58, 162

L

lamb 44, 140, 196, 200, 204
    Rack of Lamb in Curry Hoisin Sauce 44
Larson, Rick 118
Le Bernardin 82
Le Coze, Maguy and Gilbert 82
Le Fournil 17, 47, 52, 176
lemons 65, 68, 70, 77, 96, 106, 128, 131, 136, 138, 140, 154, 158, 161, 210, 211
    Cedar Plank Salmon with Preserved Lemon, Black Bean and Chive Butter 68
    Huckleberry Lemon Pudding Cake 106
    Preserved Lemons 68, 154, 161, 211
    Roasted Radishes with Blueberries and Preserved Lemons 161
    Spinach Cilantro Lemon Pesto 210
lentils
    Black Beluga Lentils 144, 147
    Green Lentils 162, 163
    Green Lentils with Grilled Nectarines and Arugula, Feta and Mint 162
    Wheat Blinis with Cowboy Caviar 144
lettuce 16, 42, 47, 124, 150, 153, 184, 187
    Butter Lettuce Salad 26, 65, 67, 150
Leuschen, Alexia and David 53
Li, Jimmy 17
Lilac Restaurant 17
Lockhart, Chris 53, 54
Loh, Lily 19, 38, 94
Luchetti, Emily 118

M

Maderal, Rochelle 189
Maplethorpe, David 16, 108, 113, 117, 118, 119
McFarren, Trevor 70, 82, 84, 85
Meyers, Scott 17, 30
Michaud, Alan 110
Montana Ale Works 109
Montana Meat Collective 110
Montana Stockgrowers Association 108
Montana Wagyu Cattle Company 109
morel mushrooms 22, 65
    James Honaker's Morel Mushroom Sherry Thyme Cream Sauce 70
    Morel Crostini 65
Morin, François 17, 47, 52, 176
Mountain Rose Herbs 105
Mowatt, Danny 53
Mueller, Kim 182
Muirhead, Mike 17, 53, 54
mushrooms 65, 70, 84, 85, 95, 96, 154, 168, 169, 200
    Green Bean Salad with Chickpeas and Brown Mushrooms 154
    James Honaker's Morel Mushroom Sherry Thyme Cream Sauce 70
    Morel Crostini 65

N

New York Restaurant School 82

nuts
  Dukkah 130, 136, **202**
  Thai Peanut Dipping Sauce 137, **201**

O

oats
  Fluffy Wheat Oatmeal Pancakes 177
Oien, David 16
onions
  Caramelized Onion Dip 206
  Caramelized Onion Jam 124, **206**
  Caramelized Onions 124, 126, 206, **207**
Ox Pasture 53

P

Parris, Daniel 56
Patent, Dorothy 106
Patent, Greg 9, 106
peaches
  Cherry Tomato Pesto Salad with Peaches and Mozzarella 153
Peck, Clint 17, 52, 168
Peter Kump's New York Cooking School 82
pheasant
  Pheasant Stir-Fry with Black Bean Sauce 34, 88, 157
Piney Dell 53, 109
polenta
  Creamy Goat Cheese Polenta 166
  Rhubarb Raspberry Polenta Cake 180
pork
  Kung Pao Pork with Red Chilies and Peanuts 38
  Pork Meatballs 47, **49**

Pork Meatballs Banh Mi Sandwiches **47**, 202
Pork Tenderloin with Huckleberry Hoisin Ginger Glaze 92, **94**
Roast Pork Chops with Grapes, Gooseberries and Rosemary 97
potatoes
  Curry Mashed Potatoes **46**, 196
  Potato Ricotta Gnocchi 172
  Smashed Potatoes with Smoked Trout 67
Prerogative Kitchen 53
Prewett, Phillip 16
Project Meats 110, 171
Pueringer, Ginnie 84
Pyburn, Reid 113, 117, 118

R

radishes
  Asparagus, Radish and Cherry Salad 62
  Roasted Radishes with Blueberries and Preserved Lemon 161
Ranch at Rock Creek, The 17, 30
Ranch House Sausage Company 16, 108, 110, 111, 112
raspberries
  Rhubarb Raspberry Polenta Cake 180
Reukauf, Lon 108, 109
Rex, The 16, 22, 108, 112, 113, 118, 119
rhubarb 106, 126, 172, 180, 203, 204
  Rhubarb Chutney 126, **204**
  Rhubarb Raspberry Polenta Cake 180
  Roasted Tomato-Rhubarb Sauce 203
rice
  Chanterelle Risotto 95
  Sweet Rice and Barley Coconut Pudding 50
Ripert, Eric 82
Rolin, James and Kathy 56, 186, 187, 189

INDEX

Rolland, Patricia 82
rose hips
   Double Chocolate Rose Hip Muffins 100
   Rose Hip Baklava 100, **102**
   Rose Hip Syrup 100, 102, **105**
Rosetto, Kate 16
Ryan, Shane 121

S

Saffron Table 17, 56
salmon 22, 42, 61, 67, 68, 122
   Cedar Planked Salmon with Preserved Lemon, Black Bean and Chive Butter 68
Schommer, Chuck 10, 13
Sherman, Sean 16
Siebert, Ken 13, 16, 56, 85, 184, 189
spinach 42, 148, 208, 210
   Spinach Caper Pesto 210
   Spinach Cilantro Lemon Pesto 210
   Spinach Pici Pasta Noodle Soup 148
Steen, Nick 16, 17, 133
Stewart, Austin 17
Sunberg, Debbie 182
Swanky Roots 16, 150, 184, 186

T

Thai Peanut Dipping Sauce 137, **201**
Thorndal, Margit 84
Timeless Natural Food 16, 144, 154, 162, 171
tomatillos
   Roasted Tomatillo Salsa 89, 142, 182, **205**
tomatoes 42, 148, 153, 184, 186, 200, 203, 205
   Cherry Tomato Pesto Salad with Peaches and Mozzarella 153
   Roasted Tomato-Rhubarb 172, **203**
Trager, Eric 53, 55, 109

trout 30, 61, 67
   Smashed Potatoes with Smoked Trout **67**, 212
   Steamed Whole Trout with Ginger and Garlic 30

U

Ulrich, Michael 17

V

Van Buskirk, Kael 189
Veronika's Pastry Shop 17, 52, 53

W

Walkers Grill 16, 17, 85, 133
Wellington, Raymond 82
Wells, Dave 30
Whistle Pig Korean 17, 41
Woods, Emma 41

Y

Yamanaka, Jackie 13, 15, 108
Yellowstone Cellars and Winery 17, 52, 75, 168
Yoon, Joseph 16, 186, 188, 189

Z

Zirotti, Laurent 82
zucchini
   Easy Zucchini Sauté 141
   Grilled Zucchini 138, 140
   Zucchini Flower Corn Soup 142
   Zucchini Noodles 140
   Zucchini Puree 140

ABOUT THE AUTHOR AND PHOTOGRAPHER

Stella Fong shares her love of food, and the creators and innovators behind it, through her radio show, *Flavors Under the Big Sky: Celebrating the Bounty of the Region* for Yellowstone Public Radio. In the twenty years she has lived in Billings, Montana, she has grown to savor the regional bounty by integrating the Chinese flavors from her childhood and world influences while learning from culinarians near and far. With a cooking certificate from the Culinary Institute of America in Hyde Park and Greystone, Stella has shared her cooking knowledge through her classes for Sur La Table, Williams-Sonoma, the Cellar at Macy's and Gelson's. After receiving a Certified Wine Professional Certification from the Culinary Institute of America, she taught the introductory classes for the Montana State University, Billings Foundation Wine and Festival.

Fong contributes regularly to *Yellowstone Valley Woman Magazine* and "The Last Best Plates" column for the *Billings Gazette* and the *Montana Standard*. Her articles have appeared in *Edible Bozeman*, the *Washington Post*, *Cooking Light*, *Fine Cooking*, *Big Sky Journal*, *Western Art and Architecture* and the *San Diego Union Tribune*. She is the author of *Historic Restaurants of Billings: A Taste of the Magic City's Past* and *Billings Food: The Flavorful Story of Montana's Trailhead*.

When Fong is not writing or cooking, she cross-country skis, sails, bikes and fly-fishes the world.

ABOUT THE AUTHOR AND PHOTOGRAPHER

Lynn Donaldson-Vermillion is a Livingston, Montana–based photojournalist whose appetite for adventure and thirst for travel have her roaming throughout the Rocky Mountains, shooting and writing about Sugar Beet Festivals, Catholic Burgers, Wild Game Cook-Offs and the absolutely best places to eat pie. Founder and creative director of the Montana food + travel blog TheLastBestPlates.com, you can find her stories and images in *National Geographic Traveler*, *Saveur*, *Travel + Leisure*, *Food & Wine*, *Sunset*, the *New York Times*, the *Wall Street Journal* and many other national publications, as well as at TheFoodNetwork.com. Lynn is also a featured Instagrammer for NatGeoTravel and has chronicled mermaid bars in Central Montana, taimen fishing in Mongolia and morel hunting in the Absaroka-Beartooth Wilderness. Her weekly newspaper column, "The Last Best Plates," appears each Wednesday in the *Billings Gazette*, the *Missoulian*, the *Montana Standard*, the *Helena Independent Record* and the *Ravalli Republic*. She shoots the "Dining Out" column, written by Seabring Davis, for *Big Sky Journal*. Donaldson-Vermillion has shot four additional cookbooks (*The Western Kitchen: Seasonal Recipes from Montana's Chico Hot Springs Resort*; *Open Range: Steaks, Chops and More from Big Sky Country*; and *New Frontier Cooking: Recipes from Montana's Mustang Kitchen*). She and her adventurer husband are raising three spirited children who love eating everything from southern barbecue and Bahamian conch to Mongolian khorkhog. When not scouring the globe in search of appetizing stories, the Vermillion family can be found on the trails and streams surrounding Livingston.

www.ingramcontent.com/pod-product-compliance
Lightning Source LLC
Chambersburg PA
CBHW060921170426
43191CB00024B/2446